Norman Schwarzkopf

Hero with a Heart

by Libby Hughes

A People in Focus Book

AN AUTHORS GUILD BACKINPRINT.COM EDITION

For Wendy, Mark, and Kathy, whose personal
and professional lives reflect a sense of ethics

Norman Schwartzkopf
Hero with a Heart
All Rights Reserved © 1992, 2002 by Libby Hughes

AN AUTHORS GUILD BACKINPRINT.COM EDITION

Published by iUniverse, Inc.

For information address:
iUniverse
2021 Pine Lake Road, Suite 100
Lincoln, NE 68512
www.iuniverse.com

Originally published by Dillon Press

Photo Credits:
Front Cover image: USAF–SSGT Dean Wagner
Back cover image: AP–Wide World Photos

AP–Wide World Photos: 8, 13, 26
Visions Photo: 16, 20, 22, 70, 74
Valley Forge Military Academy: 34, 39
Department of Defense–
    USAF–MSGT Ken Hammond: 81

U. S. Army: 87, 110
Harry Benson: 96, 105, 134
USAF: 99
USAF–SSGT Dean Wagner: 125
USAF–MSGT Thompson: 131

ISBN: 0-595-25570-1

Printed in the United States of America

Acknowledgments

With gratitude to Ambassador and Mrs. Walter Annenberg for opening the way to the Valley Forge Military Academy and Marion Clewell for her navigational talents and hospitality. Special thanks to: Larry Edwards, Admiral N. Ronald Thunman, Michelle Deveney, and Cadet Jim Springer at VFMA; also, Major General Richard A. Freytag; Susan and Jim Hug, along with Chuck Windsor for the channel to West Point. The United States Military Academy at West Point couldn't have been more cooperative: Major James D. Peterson, Colonel Bell, Colonel James Hawthorne, Ray Aalbue and his photographs, Annebette McElrice. Special thanks to former West Point Superintendent General Dave R. Palmer, General John C. "Doc" Bahnsen and Lt. Colonel Peggy Bahnsen, Colonel Terry Hand, Special Library Collections and the Archives at West Point, and Ted Halligan. USMA photos by Army Lt. Bianco, Mr. and Mrs. Buccanfuso, Bill Dwyer, and Gordon Buxton of Lawrenceville, New Jersey; Betsy Bevis (of Stewart, Florida), Mary C. Clarke (of Pennington, New Jersey); Mary Howe Thompson of Manchester, Vermont; Captain B. Gallagher and Sergeant Tom De Feo of the New Jersey State Police; Betty Barker at the Trenton Library archives; Harold.Elliot; Bill Wells of Bordentown, New Jersey. With thanks to the Pentagon for their cooperation: especially Captain Barbara Goodno, Charles A. Chase, Lt. Colonel Makara, Colonel Mo Faber, and General Schwarzkopf's secretaries. At the Army War College in Carlisle, Pennsylvania: Lt. Colonel Larry Icenogle, Colonel Donald E. Lunday, and Colonel John Counts. At Ft. Lewis: Norman Neubert and Kenneth Greenwood; at Ft. Richardson, Charles Canterbury; Virginia Johnson in Anchorage for introducing me to General Norman Wood. Major Ed Gribbins and Captain Ida McGrath at Ft. Campbell, Kentucky. Janet B. Wray and John Head at Ft. Leavenworth, Kansas. At Ft. Stewart, Dean Wohlgemuth, Mrs. Jane Tutten, Dennis and Martha Grice, William Montcrief, and Odis W. King. Schwarzkopf's roommates from West Point: General Leroy N. Suddath and David Finch Horton. At Ft. Benning, General Kenneth C. Leuer, Al Garland, Al Blanchard, Sergeant Springman. Thanks to Patricia White of Grenada and Ted Morse, Director of USAID in Zimbabwe. At Shaw Air Force Base, Captain Tom Barth. Major Martin Compton and Colonel Randy Conklin of Central Command. Thanks to Charlotte Agee and Edith Russell for bringing me together with Will Hill Tankersley, who introduced me to General Khaled bin Sultan bin Abdulaziz. Alabama residents and 1956 West Point graduates: Kenneth Knowles and Richard Adams. Dr. Robert K. Wright, Jr.—historian at the Center for Military History. Evan Duncan, office of the historian, Department of State. Bill and Gret Pockman for their clipping services. Barrie and Paul Hewitt for introducing me to Jamal Al Thani. As always, Betty and John Saunders of California.

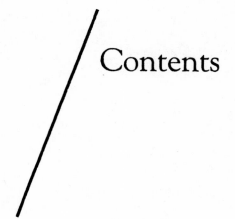

Contents

General H. Norman Schwarzkopf and his wife, Brenda, wave
to the crowds during the ticker tape parade celebrating the swift
victory in the Persian Gulf.

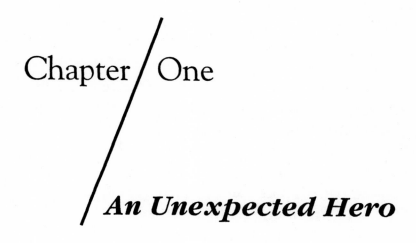

Chapter / One

An Unexpected Hero

A big, bearlike man in camouflage fatigues sat on the back of an open convertible. He was riding in a parade down New York City's lower Broadway on a hot June day in 1991. Over 6,000 tons of shredded paper floated down on him to celebrate the swift victory in the Persian Gulf. With pieces of confetti landing on his cotton bucket cap, he smiled, waved, and seemed not to notice.

This was four-star General H. Norman Schwarzkopf.

He had become an international hero as the military architect of Desert Shield/Desert Storm. These were two military operations waged in the Middle East. Desert Shield was the military preparation for the defense of Saudi Arabia from Iraq

from August 7, 1990, through January 16, 1991.
Desert Storm was the actual military attack against
Iraq from January 17, 1991, until the cease-fire on
February 28, 1991. The purpose of Desert Storm
was to drive Iraqi forces out of the small country of
Kuwait, which had been invaded by Iraq on August
2, 1990. President Saddam Hussein of Iraq had
ordered the invasion. He wanted Kuwait's rich oil
fields for Iraq. The United States, along with 27
allied countries, was the major player in the operation to drive Hussein out of Kuwait.

Until the Persian Gulf War, General Norman
Schwarzkopf was virtually unknown to those outside the United States Army. To those who did
know him, his success was not a surprise. The qual-
ities of leadership, gritty determination, and quick
wit had been visible in the teenager at Valley Forge
Military Academy and in the young cadet at West
Point. Those formative years, together with 35
years of assorted military assignments, had molded
a hero.

Thrust into the limelight through his articu-
late briefings for reporters and the American public
on television, General Schwarzkopf became an

instant celebrity. There were numerous interviews by the media, exploring his background and career.

Schwarzkopf's ancestors had lived in Würtemberg, Germany. Christian Schwarzkopf, Norman's great-grandfather, had dreamed of going to America for adventure and opportunity. As a teenager in 1853, he boarded a ship and sailed to New York City. Trained as a jeweler, Christian settled in Newark, New Jersey, where many jewelry designers and goldsmiths worked at the time.

Norman's father, Herbert Norman Schwarzkopf, was born in Newark. He was the only son of a very close-knit German family who spoke their native language at home. General Schwarzkopf's father was a colorful character who would become the greatest influence in his life.

Father and son had similar careers. Norman's father left home for a military boarding school at the age of nine. By 17, he was enrolled at West Point. He graduated in the class of 1917, trained as a cavalry officer.

From West Point, his father went to fight on the battlefields of France against the Germans in World War I. An enemy attack of mustard gas cut short his combat experience. When his parents became seriously ill, the elder Schwarzkopf was forced to resign from military life to return to New Jersey to take care of them.

From 1921 to 1936, he was chief of the New Jersey State Police. His reputation was one of firmness and compassion. During this period, he met and married Norman's mother, Ruth Alice Bowman, a trained nurse. They had two daughters, Ruth Ann and Sally, born two years apart. The family lived in the small town of Pennington, New Jersey.

Norman's father achieved unexpected national fame when he was named chief investigator in the Lindbergh kidnapping case. Charles A. Lindbergh had become a world hero in 1927 when he flew nonstop across the Atlantic Ocean from New York to Paris. On a windy March night in 1932, a kidnapper climbed to a second-story bedroom of the Lindbergh house in Hopewell, New Jersey, and snatched their 20-month-old son from his crib. The kidnapping stunned the world, which was plunged into grief when the baby's body was found in the woods. During the trial of the accused kid-

As head of the New Jersey State Police, Norman Schwarzkopf, Sr., talks to reporters about the Lindbergh kidnapping case.

napper, Bruno Hauptmann, the Schwarzkopfs befriended the Lindberghs.

On August 22, 1934, Mrs. Schwarzkopf gave birth to a son. The boy was delivered by Dr. Henry Rowan at Mercer Hospital in Trenton, New Jersey. The elder Schwarzkopf had wanted a son, and his two daughters were pleased to have a brother, too.

The proud father was confident that the name

Schwarzkopf would be carried into future genera-
tions by his new son—H. Norman Schwarzkopf.
Because the elder Schwarzkopf had never liked the
name Herbert, he gave his son only the initial H
and not the name attached to it.

While the Schwarzkopfs were still living in
Pennington, they frequently visited their friends.
Mary Howe, who was only four at the time,
remembered the elder Schwarzkopf in his riding
breeches and shiny boots. "He was a very dashing-
looking man," said the woman, who is now mayor
of Manchester, Vermont. "My mother remarked
that little Norman was a cheery, rather plump
baby."

With the Schwarzkopf family growing, the
white Pennington house soon became too small. In
their search for a new home, they found a beautiful
gray-stone house in Lawrenceville, New Jersey,
only five or six miles from Pennington and next to
the green, tree-filled university town of Princeton.

On the outskirts of Lawrenceville and Princeton, the farmlands fan out in endless flat stretches.
Near the loop around the Gothic buildings of
Princeton University are clusters of trees. The
town of Princeton merges into Lawrenceville on

that circular drive. Lawrenceville was a peaceful, rural village, famous for the Lawrenceville Preparatory School for Boys, founded in 1810. The American revolutionary forces trekked through the fields in this area between 1777 and 1779.

This was an ideal location for the Schwarzkopfs. Their gray-stone house with green shutters at 2549 Main Street had been built in 1815. At one time, it was a dormitory for the prep school. A thick-trunked purple beech tree still dominates the front yard, and there is a slender-limbed elm on the other side of the front sidewalk. Carved into the bark of the beech tree are many initials of previous owners. The elder Schwarzkopf added his and his wife's to a century of others.

From their front yard, the Schwarzkopfs looked across at the soccer fields through the iron fence that enclosed the redbrick buildings and gray-stone dormitories of the prep school.

The Schwarzkopf children had many neighborhood friends. Since Norman and his sister Sally were only two years apart, they were playmates. They developed a closeness that has remained throughout the years. While they were playing cowboys and Indians, their older sister, Ruth Ann,

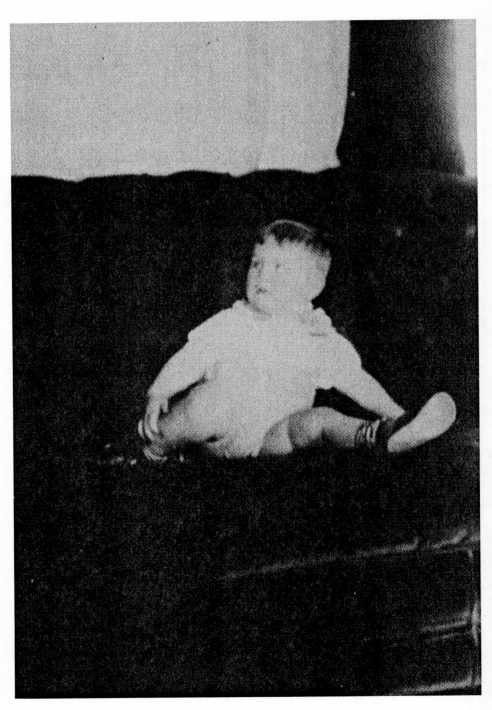

Norman at age two

was going out with boys. Gordon Buxton, one of her friends, remembers taking Ruth Ann to a movie and Boy Scout function, but getting back late. Afraid of the elder Schwarzkopf, Buxton telephoned him the next day to apologize. Ruth Ann's younger brother, Norman, just seemed like an annoying pest to Buxton.

Young Norman's childhood was a happy one. He could walk down Main Street to the grocer's little store and buy penny candy. The Lawrenceville Elementary School on Craven Street was several blocks away on a dead-end road. Behind its stone walls, Norman attended classes through third grade. On weekends, his father barbecued steaks for the family in the backyard, hidden by high hedges. After the glare of publicity from the Lindbergh case, the elder Schwarzkopf sought privacy for himself and his family.

For complicated political reasons, the elder Schwarzkopf's contract as superintendent of the New Jersey State Police was not renewed in 1936. Instead, he became the announcer on popular radio shows such as "Gangbusters," "Terry and the Pirates," and "Dick Tracy." Families across the nation gathered around their radios every night to

listen to shows like these. The Schwarzkopf name
had become famous through the Lindbergh kidnapping. Now the voice of the elder Schwarzkopf
became just as famous. But after the Middlesex
Trucking Company hired him and eventually made
him president, the elder Schwarzkopf gave up his
radio career.

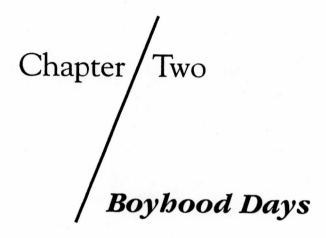

Chapter / Two

Boyhood Days

Events in the world changed the family life of the Schwarzkopfs. When Hitler's German army started World War II in 1939, the elder Schwarzkopf's military instincts drew him back to the army. In 1940, he signed on as a lieutenant colonel in New Jersey's National Guard. He was soon made a colonel of the 113th Infantry. The Schwarzkopf children would have an absent father for much of the next ten years.

Young Norman's schooling shifted and changed many times—like that of the sons and daughters in any military family. After Lawrenceville Elementary School, he attended fourth and fifth grades at the Princeton Elementary School on Nassau Street, which was also within walking dis-

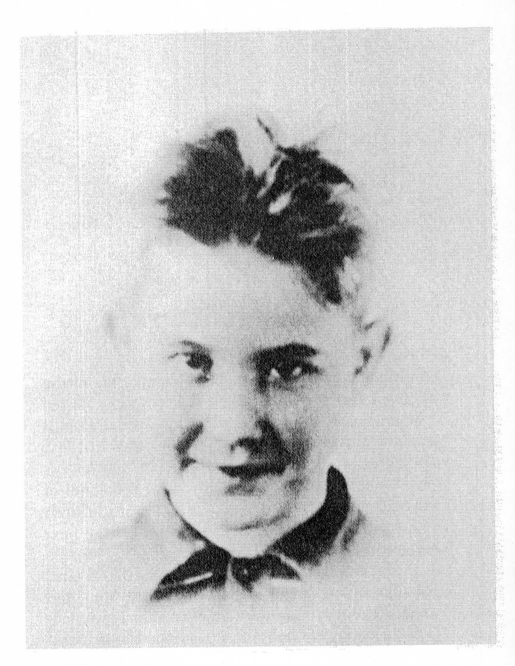

Norman at age five

tance of his house. The Bianco twins remember Norm from this school. Lieutenant Bianco of the Princeton police said, "Norm was taller than any other kid. His blond hair was slicked back. He played soccer and had an impressive bearing, but never used it to push people around."

In 1942, Norman's father received an assignment that would influence all the family members' lives. The State Department was told by President Franklin D. Roosevelt to ask Colonel Schwarzkopf to organize and train the imperial police force in Iran, a country that the United States had befriended in 1911. The new shah, Mohammed Riza Pahlavi, had several concerns for his country. First, Germany had invaded many countries in Europe and was looking greedily at Iran, with its oil and its port access to the Persian Gulf. Second, Iran and its cities were out of control. The country was in chaos. Furthermore, the Russian supply line of oil through Iran had to be protected from German invaders.

After a two-month briefing in Washington, D.C., Colonel Schwarzkopf left his family in New Jersey and went to Tehran, the capital of Iran, to begin his duties. From 1942 to 1946, the colonel

was stationed in Iran. Because he was very devoted
to his family, this separation was very difficult for
him. He wrote them long letters, describing the
people and culture—even drawing pictures to show
them what he was seeing. Every letter was a
romantic adventure for the three Schwarzkopf children as they listened to their mother read about
the distant desert land.

On his travels, Colonel Schwarzkopf bought
art objects from the bazaars in Iran and sent them
to the family for Christmas and birthdays. For Norman's tenth birthday, his father carefully selected a
300-year-old Persian ax. His message to his son
read: "I find joy and significance in giving you this
for your tenth birthday and consider it a prediction
of your worthy success in the 'battle of life.'"

While the colonel was training the Iranian
police force, Mrs. Schwarzkopf held their family
together. Because of her nursing background, she
volunteered for the American Red Cross, but taking care of her three children was a full-time occupation. In 1945 the Schwarzkopfs decided that
Norman should go to military school as his father
before him had. Young Norman attended sixth
grade at the Bordentown Military Institute, not
many miles away from home.

Colonel Schwarzkopf was sent to Iran to organize and advise the Iranian National Police.

BMI was set on a hill near the banks of the Delaware River. Its white, 19th-century buildings were surrounded by athletic fields where the 300 cadets marched and drilled in their khaki uniforms and visored caps. As the institute grew, many of the boys had to live in one of six wooden houses across the street.

At BMI, the boys learned respect for elders, courtesy, scholarship, and punctuality. For breaking rules, guard duty was imposed. On Sundays, the cadets would march through town in their dress gray uniforms to go to church.

Bordentown, New Jersey, was a historic place. Thomas Paine, writer and American patriot, had lived there. Francis Hopkinson, one of the signers of the Declaration of Independence, had also been one of its residents. Clara Barton, founder of the American Red Cross in 1881, had lived down the street from the institute at one time. Joseph Bonaparte, who had negotiated a treaty with the United States for France, had lived in Bordentown from 1815 to 1841. In addition, Bordentown claimed to be the first town to make and sell ice cream, an idea imported from France.

When Norman posed for his youthful cadet

photograph, his mother encouraged him to smile. He wouldn't. If he was to become a general, he wanted to look serious. Therefore, he stubbornly stood unsmiling before the camera. However, the untamed hair and hint of mischief in the eyes and at the corners of his mouth belied his serious expression.

During the years her husband was away, Ruth Schwarzkopf was in charge of bringing up and disciplining her children. Although she came from West Virginia, her views on racial issues were not those of many southerners. She believed in equality for all people, whatever their religion, age, or race. She taught her children to give up their seats on public transportation to elderly people.

One day, when Norman was less than ten years old, he was riding a bus. When he saw an elderly black woman standing in the aisle, he stood up and offered her his seat. Many people around him laughed. Puzzled by this reaction, he told his mother about the incident. She replied, "Remember this: You were born white. You were born Protestant. You were born an American. Therefore, you are going to be spared prejudices other people will not be spared. But you should never forget one

Norman relaxes in a lawn chair with his dog.

thing: You had absolutely nothing to do with the fact that you were born that way. It was an accident of birth that spared you this prejudice." Norman never forgot this piece of advice.

His mother's stand on equality extended to Norman's schoolmates as well. She taught Norman and his sisters that they should treat all people fairly, whether they were rich or poor, black or white.

During his father's absence, Norman took up a hobby. He became interested in magic tricks and sent away for magicians' kits. For hours, he practiced sleight of hand. He refused to show anyone how the tricks were done, true to the magician's code.

By the summer of 1946, Norman had finished his first year at BMI. Even though the war in Europe and Asia was over, his father was still in Iran and was very homesick for his family. The elder Schwarzkopf felt it was now safe for them to join him in the Middle East. He sent first for Norman, and later for his daughters and his wife.

Together, the military father and the 12-year-old son explored the Persian gardens and the open bazaars with their exotic sights and aromas. They

enjoyed riding horseback and going on hunting
expeditions to the mountains, where the father
taught the son to shoot a rifle. On these hunting
trips, they were sometimes the guests of mountain
tribesmen. Norman learned from his father to
accept hospitality graciously and to eat whatever
was served to him, even sheep's eyes. He learned to
respect the religion of Islam and to speak a few
words of the Farsi language. This early experience
would be invaluable in H. Norman Schwarzkopf's
leadership in the Persian Gulf War 44 years later.

Once the whole Schwarzkopf family was
reunited, they moved into a big house with many
servants in the diplomatic center of Tehran. The
parents insisted that the children not order the servants to run errands for them or to clean up after
them. They did not want their three children to
become spoiled.

After months of being a companion to his
father, it was time for Norman to enter school
again. He skipped seventh grade and went into
eighth grade at the Presbyterian Missionary School
in Tehran. His sisters also went there.

But soon the idyllic days in Iran came to an
end.

Chapter / Three

Europe and Valley Forge Military Academy

The Schwarzkopfs were faced with a problem. The missionary school in Tehran went only through the tenth grade. Sally and Ruth Ann would have to go somewhere else for high school. Their parents decided to put all three children in the École Internationale in Geneva, Switzerland. Much as their father did not want to give up the companionship of his children, he thought their education was more important. All three children became boarders. Norman entered ninth grade and began to learn French and German. He enjoyed sports, particularly soccer and skiing.

Once the now brigadier general Schwarzkopf had completed his mission of training and updating the Iranian police force, he resumed his military career in Europe, where he was posted from 1948 to 1950. His first assignment was to Frankfurt, Germany. When World War II ended in 1945, the American military had remained in Germany as part of the Allied peace agreement, which also included British, French, and Russian military presence.

Young Norman was not studying as hard in Geneva as he should have been, so his father brought him to Frankfurt to enter tenth grade in an American school set up for the children of military personnel.

In another move to Heidelberg, Germany, the elder Schwarzkopf was assigned to the army police as its provost marshal. Young Norman was soon in another school for American students. In 11th grade, he became a football player on his school's championship team.

During the two assignments in Germany, the brigadier general traveled much of the time. While he was away, he expected his children to follow the rules of the Schwarzkopf household. One of the rules was a weekend midnight curfew for the teenage Norman. Because he was gregarious and fun loving, Norman would sometimes come in later than the set hour. On one such occasion, Norman was grounded as punishment. He went up to his room and played "Home, Sweet Home" over and over again on his accordion until his mother couldn't stand it any longer and released him from his confinement.

In 1950, Norman's father was stationed in Rome to be in charge of the Military Assistance Advisory Group for Italy. Although Italy was an attractive assignment, father and son jointly decided on a change in Norman's educational career. Norman wanted to follow in his father's footsteps and go to West Point, but the schooling in Europe was not adequate preparation. Since the elder Schwarzkopf knew the reputation of Valley Forge Military Academy in Wayne, Pennsylvania, he wrote for an application. Norman would have to repeat 11th grade, but since he had skipped seventh, this would not be a hardship. His two sisters were already back in the United States at Smith and Wellesley colleges.

The very name *Valley Forge* summons up historic memories. One of the harshest winters in the American revolutionary war was spent on the rolling hills and valleys of Valley Forge, Pennsylva-

nia. In 1777 and 1778, the terrible weather, the
shortage of food, and the lack of clothing had chal-
lenged George Washington's troops. Only the
troops' loyalty and training by Baron Friedrich Wil-
helm von Steuben gave the soldiers courage to sur-
vive the winter and hold the line against the
British.

Barely a dozen miles from Valley Forge is
Wayne, Pennsylvania. The town was named after
Mad Anthony Wayne, one of the leaders of the
American revolutionary forces at Valley Forge.
Along the 120 acres of the Valley Forge Military
Academy (VFMA) runs a narrow and bumpy road.
This was one of many wagon trails worn and
grooved by the early settlers. The academy itself
was started in 1928 by General Milton G. Baker.
Before it burned down, the school held its classes
in a large, old-fashioned hotel. Author J. D.
Salinger, playwright Edward Albee, Senator War-
ren Rudman, and musician James Sturr are some of
the distinguished graduates. The name of Schwarzkopf has been added to that list.

The bushy maple and oak trees inside the iron
fence enclosing the academy were like those at the
Lawrenceville school near Norman's old home.

The grounds of this school, though, were much hillier and more rugged than those of Lawrenceville. Serpentine sidewalks connected the tidy brick and white-columned buildings that ran along a long slope. At the bottom of the slope was the grand parade ground for formal marches and parades on Sundays and special occasions.

Despite his travels and eclectic schooling in Iran and Europe, Norman felt at home in the academy atmosphere. Because of his days at Bordentown Military Institute, the military life-style was comfortable to him. He respected VFMA's motto: Courage, Honor, Conquer. The 6'3", 200-pound Norman entered VFMA on a football scholarship. If he wanted to be accepted at West Point, he had to maintain high grades. With an IQ of 170, this was not difficult for Norman.

Soon he settled into Wheeler Hall barracks on the first floor. The windows of his corner dormitory room looked up at the newly constructed chapel whose white spire dominated all the other buildings. His room, with iron bunk beds, wooden closet, cubbyholes, and desks, was shared with one roommate for sleep and study over the next two years.

Norman served as tackle on the football team at Valley Forge Military Academy.

On Mondays, Wednesdays, and Fridays, Norman was required to wear his blue-and-gray dress uniform. On Tuesdays and Thursdays, green camouflage fatigues were worn. At 5:30, the morning bugle call, or reveille, awakened him. After dressing, making his bed, and cleaning his room, he joined the other cadets outside and fell into formation for roll call and the march to the mess hall for breakfast. At 7:00, details (cleaning jobs) were executed by new cadets but overseen by sergeants and cadet officers.

At the next bugle call, Norman and the other cadets marched to classes in Shannon Hall—diagonally up the hill from Wheeler Hall. On either side of the shiny linoleum-floored hallways and cream-colored walls were the classrooms. Classes of 10 or 15 students sat at long tables with straight-backed chairs. Ballpoint pens were not yet in common use, so there was a round inkwell hole in the upper right-hand corner of each desk. The smell of black ink and blackboard chalk was ever present.

Except for lunch at noon, classes were in session until 3:00 P.M. From 4:00 to 6:00 P.M., drills, military maneuvers, sports, and extracurricular activities were scheduled on specific days. Norman,

however, could always find time for a quick stop at
the snack bar known as the Boodle Shop. After
dinner, the bugle call signaled cadets to study in
their rooms with books open from 7:30 to 9:30.
Taps, or lights out, was 10:00 P.M. for everyone but
seniors, who were permitted another hour of study
time.

For violating the rules, cadets were made to
walk penalty tours back and forth on the paved
area outside Wheeler Hall. In the depths of winter,
this was a dreaded punishment. Once, Cadet
Schwarzkopf found himself pacing the quadrangle
for getting into a food fight in the mess hall. His
Christmas vacation was in jeopardy for this breach
of rules. A letter from the superintendent permitted him to go home but warned him to think seriously about his misdeed.

Life at VFMA was not all work. Sometimes
Norman went into the town of Wayne and walked
over the hump of its main street to eat ice cream
and browse in the quaint stores. On occasional
weekends, Norman took the train to Maplewood,
New Jersey, where his parents had purchased a two-
story white house on Washington Street when his
father returned from Europe in 1951.

There were opportunities for Norman to participate in many activities and achieve success as a leader. Edward Hausberg, a classmate of Norman's, remembered him this way: "He accomplished more in two years than most people do in six or seven. He was well liked by everybody and had a sense of humor. He was my first sergeant when I was a company commandant. He hasn't changed that much."

On the football field, Norman was a lineman and his team won five out of eight games. He also heaved the shot-put on the track team. Norman was a class treasurer and won the Eric Fisher Wood Chapter of the National Honor Society for scholarship, character, leadership, and service. As one of the best debaters, he won the Dunaway Debate Award for debating the topic "That the federal government should institute a permanent system of price and wage controls." For his journalistic excellence, Norman added Quills and Scrolls to his list of awards.

Although Norman was editor of the yearbook, *Crossed Sabres*, his staff mischievously sabotaged his own biography by slipping in a description of the *H* in his name. They wrote that his name was Hugo. This, of course, was not true, and Norman was angry to see it in print. His friends had teased him unmercifully about the H in front of his name.

By the end of May 1952, the dogwoods were in full bloom, and the maple leaves fluttered in the soft breezes. Graduation time had arrived. General and Mrs. H. Norman Schwarzkopf would watch their son give the valedictory address from the pulpit of the new chapel of St. Cornelius the Centurion. Because his grades were the highest in the class, Norman was named as valedictorian. General George C. Marshall and Ambassador Walter Annenberg were among the guests that year who heard the tall, fair-haired cadet deliver his farewell in his blue-gray uniform.

Cadet Schwarzkopf's speech was sincere but brief. He looked back with warmth at the years at Valley Forge Military Academy and expressed gratitude for what the cadets had learned from academics and the military system. He and his classmates had entered as boys and were leaving as men. He paid tribute to the staff and singled out the military science and tactical department for preparing and training the cadets to preserve freedom.

Lieutenant Colonel John Stewart Mulkerns had been Norman's tactical officer. Across his pic-

Cadet H. Norman Schwarzkopf, valedictorian of his graduating class

ture in the yearbook, Norman inscribed these words to Mulkerns: "Sir, thank you so much for everything. I will never forget the training you gave me."

For Norman, the sadness of leaving close friends was offset by the fact that he had been appointed to West Point.

In 1989, Schwarzkopf said, "West Point prepared me for the army, but Valley Forge prepared me for life."

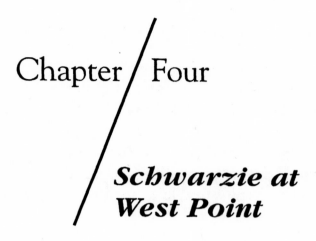

Chapter / Four

Schwarzie at West Point

West Pointers usually considered military prep schools like VFMA "tin schools" because they weren't "the real thing." They were merely schools for boys who were playing at soldiering. West Point, on the other hand, aimed to train professional army officers and provide them with an excellent education.

For Norman, the academy was a dream come true. He would follow in the footsteps of his father and join the long line of West Point graduates, who proudly wore the handsome gray uniforms with the distinctive black stripe on the outside seams of their dress trousers.

In 1952 the month of June in Maplewood, New Jersey, went by quickly for Norman and his family. His father had come back from Europe in

1951 to be in charge of New Jersey's public safety
and law enforcement division. By 1953, though, he
was drawn back to Iran to help the CIA persuade
the young shah to overthrow the Iranian government and establish his own ruling power. At least
the elder Schwarzkopf was able to see his son enter
West Point.

At the beginning of July, young Norman
packed his suitcase and left for West Point, 50
miles north of New York City. Palisades Parkway,
north of the George Washington Bridge, follows
the line of the Hudson River to Bear Mountain
Park, winding down to the rocky park of lakes and
trails only a few miles from the academy.

More than an hour after leaving Maplewood,
Norman entered the village of Highland Falls. The
narrow main street of shops and restaurants had an
old-world look—almost like that of a small German town. At the end of main street was a guard-
house in the form of a stocky stone tower.

Beyond this entrance were 116,000 acres of
rolling grounds above the jagged cliffs overlooking
the Hudson River. This was West Point, home of
the United States Military Academy. Inside the
main entrance, the Thayer Hotel, built in 1926,

appeared more like a baron's castle on the Rhine than a hotel on the Hudson.

The academy has almost two centuries of history. In 1802, President Thomas Jefferson authorized an act of Congress to establish a corps of engineers at the United States Military Academy. Some of the engineers who built America's canals, roads, and bridges were trained at the academy. In 1779, George Washington waged a strategic battle there against the British during the revolutionary war. Washington ordered a 150-ton chain to be stretched from the banks of West Point to the other side of the Hudson River to stop the British ships. Parts of the chain are still displayed on the grounds.

Cadet H. Norman Schwarzkopf began his cadet basic training, or beast barracks, on a hot, sticky July day. Although freshmen cadets could not leave the West Point grounds for eleven months, Norman was not troubled by homesickness. Christmas would be spent in barracks only for his first, or plebe, year, but he could tolerate that regulation. Unlike many other new candidates, Norman often had been away from home both in the United States and Europe.

To have been selected for West Point was an honor. Nominations for candidates had to come from senators and congressmen from each state. Academically, the nominee had to be in the top 5 to 10 percent of his class and show well-rounded experience in other activities. The four years at West Point were paid for by the federal government in exchange for at least five years of service in the army. Most graduates intended to make the army a full-time career, and this was certainly Norman Schwarzkopf's plan.

The first eight weeks were devoted completely to beast barracks. At the Arvin Gymnasium, Norman was issued army clothing, had his hair cropped short, and was measured for his dress uniform. Out on the tarmac in the Central Area, the senior cadets yelled instructions at the plebes.

"Drop your bag, mister," shouted the senior cadets.

The new cadets were taught how to march, how to salute, and how to answer officers. This was part of the military training.

"Yes, sir."

"No, sir."

"No excuse, sir."

"I don't understand, sir."

These were the four standard answers every plebe learned that day. The shouting (which changed to quiet instruction in 1986) was deafening. But by the end of the day, more than 700 new cadets would be marching in unison across the grassy parade ground to Trophy Point. There, they took the oath of allegiance to support the Constitution of the United States. The purpose of West Point was taken seriously by Norman: to provide the nation with leaders of character to serve the common defense.

Norman was assigned to First Division barracks, a four-story, fortresslike building in the Central Area. According to height, each cadet was attached to a company of 100. Those who were 6'2" and taller, called flankers, belonged to the A-1 company. The shorter cadets, or runts, were the M-1 company. Norman was definitely a flanker.

On the first floor, he shared a room with two taller young men. Their cadet quarters had once housed the distinguished Douglas MacArthur, who graduated in 1903. Norman would live with the same two roommates for four years. Leroy Newton Suddath, from Savannah, Georgia, had a soft southern drawl. His father before him had lived in the same room. David Finch Horton, from North Carolina, was fun loving and could talk as fast as he ran. All three were compatible and shared memorable times, both happy and hard, throughout the four years.

"West Point was a brotherhood to us. We bonded because of its ideals—duty, honor, country," said Suddath before their 35th West Point reunion.

Norman and his roommates expected tough treatment in beast barracks. The senior cadets would order them to march at double time up and down the stairs or to brush their teeth while saluting. At any time, the plebes might be ordered to do 30 push-ups or 40 squat jumps. After hikes of 10 to 12 miles a day, food might be withheld from them or they might have to sit at attention—chin tucked in and shoulders back—at the end of each dining table in the mess hall.

By the time the academic year began at the end of August, Norman and the other plebes were hardened and conditioned. They had learned to obey orders instantly. Their days started before 6:00 A.M. and ended at 11:00 P.M. Classes were held five and a half days a week. Saturday afternoon was for marching, and attendance at chapel on Sunday morning was compulsory. (It wasn't until 1972 that attendance became voluntary.)

Because West Point had always been famous for training and producing fine engineers, most of the courses were oriented toward mathematics. Norman had a range of math and engineering classes, English, history, a language (usually German or French for him), military history, and courses relating to weaponry. Computers, even as early as the 1950s, were used for military technology.

Norman and his fellow cadets were expected to go to the boards (blackboards) and to recite every day. These performances were graded, and the average of those grades was posted every week.

Some afternoons (from 3:00 to 5:30 P.M.) were devoted to varsity and intramural sports. Although Norman had been a star linebacker at VMFA, he had greater competition at West Point and didn't make varsity. A knee injury kept him from participating in the intramural league. Wrestling and soccer, though, brought him athletic recognition.

One of Norman's close friends, John C. "Doc" Bahnsen, recalled: "Norm had a powerful kick. He

West Point

played goalie and could kick the length of the field.
The only way to beat him was to figure out where
not to kick it so that Norm would not pick it up.
He was like a one-man team."

Within the confinement of their barracks
room, Schwarzie, Leroy, and Dave were adjusting
to each other and to their surroundings. They
decided to take turns rotating from the single bed
to the bunk beds. For inspection, they were taught

how to fold their clothes, make their beds, and clean their room.

After every Christmas, cadets traditionally fell into a gloom period. Everything at West Point was gray—from the buildings and the uniforms to the trees and sky. However, Norman, Leroy, and Dave had ways of combating this depressing time.

"The three of us read out loud together to break the monotony of bleak winters. We enjoyed reading *Huckleberry Finn*. Schwarzie loved reading poetry. All of us liked listening to classical music, and Schwarzkopf understood it. We memorized A. E. Housman's poem for elocution and critiqued each other," said David Horton.

The poem was "Here Dead Lie We Because We Did Not Choose."

> Here dead lie we because we did not choose
> To live and shame the land from which we sprung.
> Life, to be sure, is nothing much to lose;
> But young men think it is, and we were young.

"All of us aspired to become generals. I thought Schwarzie would become one. We discussed classic battles waged by generals such as Hannibal, Xerxes, and Alexander the Great. Norm was bright and hardly ever studied. He would review his subject twenty minutes before going to class and get high grades," recalled Leroy Suddath.

Although Norman's academic record placed him forty-second in a graduating class of four hundred eighty-five, his friends and professors thought he could have been among the top five. But Schwarzkopf liked many extracurricular activities—sports, choir, and the German club. The academic competition at West Point also was greater than at Valley Forge Military Academy because of the high scholastic qualifications of the cadets.

During the following summer, as a sophomore, or "yearling," Norman trained at Camp Buckner, five miles from West Point. Here, he trained in night-raid tactics and maneuvers. One classmate recalled an incident from that summer: "Somebody did not turn up for duty at his camp at the right time or place when Norman was company commander. Norman reprimanded him for not being there to perform his duties. The man said that he had arranged for someone else to stand in for him. At that point, Norman lost his temper and berated the young man for not taking responsibility to see that his replacement was there or to take it himself."

The Schwarzkopf hot temper became legendary throughout his career. In a television interview with Barbara Walters, General Schwarzkopf acknowledged that he was not proud of his temper. He cited his first tour in Vietnam as the time this flaw developed. Others have referred to the incident at West Point as a small preview. Still others have said that the Schwarzkopf temper was something he used, or staged, to get things done.

One of the favorite outside activities for many cadets was the choir. Everyone auditioned. "I sang my lungs out," said David Horton. "But I didn't make it. Norm did. He became leader of the choir and went on many of the envied trips away from West Point."

Unlike his father, young Norman never received any demerits that would penalize him with a walking tour on the Central Area. For any misbehavior or violation of rules, the cadets had to march back and forth on the paved area for a specified number of hours. While at Valley Forge, Norman had been punished this way for his food fight.

Since time was so precious for studies and sports at West Point, this was an effective punishment. Only once did Norman come close. While in Philadelphia at the Army/Navy football game, he missed the roll call formation at the train station. Norman expected a stiff penalty, but Ethiopia's Emperor Haile Selassie was visiting West Point and granted amnesty to all students that day. There was a rule that if any member of a royal family pardoned you, you wouldn't be punished.

During his years as a junior (cow) and senior (firstie), Norman and his classmates rode the train to New York City for weekends. Often they stayed at the Astor and Piccadilly hotels, went to Broadway shows, and ate at Mamma Leone's, a favorite of West Point cadets since Eisenhower's day in 1915.

In March of 1956, graduating cadets in Norman's class could choose their branch of service. Infantry was the least favored, but Norman Schwarzkopf decided he wanted to be a ground pounder, or grunt, and persuaded others to join him.

Though the four years were coming to an end, Norman's loyalty to West Point would never flag.

Norman's senior yearbook photo at West Point in 1956

The words of the West Point motto—Duty, Honor, Country—were written on his heart. When Norman graduated from West Point in 1956, it was a proud moment for his parents, particularly for his father. Many great generals had gone to West Point: Omar N. Bradley, Ulysses S. Grant, John J. Pershing, Douglas MacArthur, George C. Patton, Dwight D. Eisenhower.

Schwarzkopf's father hoped his son would also become a general.

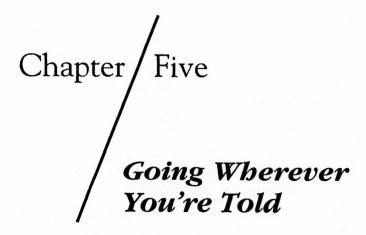

Chapter / Five

Going Wherever You're Told

With West Point behind him, newly commissioned Second Lieutenant H. Norman Schwarzkopf began a long voyage into a 35-year military career.

Many have described life in the military as a religion. They say it demands the head, heart, soul, and body of each soldier and officer. From the time Norman was four years old, he knew that he was destined to give his all to the army. With that decision would come hardships. The pay was low. He would be constantly moving to different military posts here and abroad. In war, he would put his life and those of others on the line. Despite these risks, Lieutenant Schwarzkopf and some of his West Point friends enthusiastically headed to their first

assignment at Fort Benning's Infantry and Ranger
School in October of 1956.

From ancient Greek times to the Persian Gulf
War, infantrymen have waged, won, and lost many
of the fiercest battles in history. There is no glam-
our attached to the lot of a foot soldier. He may
have to slog through mud, swamps, sand, and
rocks, and up mountains and through valleys. He
may face unpredictable weather changes. He may
face starvation and have to eat food rations in a
foxhole for months. He must be prepared to weep
over friends lost in battle. He must reconcile his
heart to missing his loved ones. But in his loneli-
ness, he fights for a purpose—to protect and defend
the freedom of others. H. Norman Schwarzkopf
was prepared to make those sacrifices.

Fort Benning, near Columbus, Georgia, strad-
dles the border with Alabama. Since 1918, the post
has been called the "home of the infantry." With
182,000 acres, the post looks more like a green-
lawned country club than a training installation for
parachutists and infantrymen. The quarters for the
soldiers and residences for high-ranking officers
were built in the 1930s and have a Spanish flavor,
with their white stucco walls and red-tiled roofs.

Some of the back roads leading to Columbus are carved into a series of roller coaster hills. The rich red earth nourishes large peach groves and sod farms. Norman Schwarzkopf would spend five months learning the techniques of physical training and parachuting there.

On Eubanks Airfield at Fort Benning, there are steel towers and wooden structures for the trainees. Lieutenant Schwarzkopf learned how to harness himself into a parachute, how to jump out of an airplane, how to operate the canopy, and how to perform a swing landing. The BIOC (Basic Infantry Officer's Course) instructed him in the skill of jumping from a 34-foot tower and a 250-foot tower. In the final week of parachuting, Norman made five good jumps from an airplane and earned his wings. A master parachutist successfully makes 65 jumps. After Norman's two tours in Vietnam, he became a master parachutist and was awarded the Distinguished Flying Cross. Furthermore, every morning, Norman and the others had to do calisthenics and run two to four miles.

There were times of leisure, too. Some of the young officers spent weekends off the post. Kenneth Leuer, a friend and fellow trainee with Norman, remembered a weekend in New Orleans when a group of them stayed with John McGinn's parents. The young men listened to jazz, ate Cajun food, and went to the horse races.

After finishing training at Fort Benning in March 1957, Lieutenant Schwarzkopf found himself at Fort Campbell, Kentucky, for two years. This military post also straddled two states, Tennessee and Kentucky, on 105,000 acres. On this rolling land of bluegrass, vineyards grew and Tennessee walking horses were bred. Near this spot, General Ulysses S. Grant had captured control of the Cumberland and Tennessee rivers from the Confederate armies during the Civil War.

Schwarzkopf assumed his first leadership role in 1957 as platoon leader of 35 men who were part of the 2nd Airborne Battle Group of the 187th Infantry. Although the new lieutenant was responsible for his platoon, his platoon sergeant actually trained the men. Therefore, Norman was directly dependent upon the sergeant to make the men look good for him. In fact, the platoon sergeant was like a mentor to the new second lieutenant.

On this Kentucky post, lined with pines and oaks, the "Screaming Eagles," who parachuted from helicopters, were trained. The nickname came from Civil War days when an eagle called Old Abe went into battle with the Union armies and screamed as the armies were about to attack. The 101st Airborne, as it was named in 1956, later trained troops first for Vietnam and then for Saudi Arabia in the Desert Shield/Storm operation.

During the time Schwarzkopf was at Fort Campbell, riots erupted in Little Rock, Arkansas, when integration was legally imposed on the public schools. Fort Campbell supplied members of the 101st Airborne to help control the situation.

For Lieutenant Norman Schwarzkopf, November 1958 brought a tremendous sorrow to his life. His father, who had retired from the army in 1956, suddenly died, and Norman returned to New Jersey for the funeral. He went there to be with his two sisters and mother before his father was buried in the West Point cemetery. One of Norman's greatest heroes had passed from the scene, but the legacy of love and character he had left behind for his son would never die.

Back at Fort Campbell, Schwarzkopf was promoted to executive officer of Company E and later, assistant to the Second Airborne Battle Group. His leadership abilities were beginning to emerge in military life as they had in school and at West Point.

Life on most military posts offers everything a small town would. There are grocery stores, banks, theaters, shops, barbers, restaurants, gymnasium facilities, churches, and elementary schools. The prices are lower than at civilian establishments. Housing and a small living allowance are provided for some officers, single people, and families. Other personnel find homes and apartments in the local communities.

In the summer of 1959, Lieutenant Schwarzkopf became a first lieutenant and was sent abroad to take a new assignment. He would be returning to the country of his teenage years—Germany. This time, the city would be Berlin, with its population of two million.

After World War II ended in 1945, the city of Berlin was divided into zones to be occupied by the four Allies: the United States, Great Britain, France, and the Soviet Union. On the eastern side of Berlin, the Soviet Union controlled 8 of the 20 districts. Many Germans did not like life under Russian occupation and escaped into the western part of Berlin, which was controlled by the other three Allies. In 1948, the Soviets tried to take over the whole of Berlin and failed. By 1961, Berlin was divided into West Berlin and East Berlin. Two concrete walls were constructed to keep the East Germans in the Russian sector from escaping to the west. Between the two walls was the death strip, guarded by dogs, tank traps, electric fences, and minefields.

During the time Norman was in Berlin, American soldiers were almost like ambassadors. Their behavior—good or bad—in the beautiful old-world city was a reflection on the United States. The German government paid all expenses for the allied troops except their salaries. The American headquarters was located in the Clay compound, which had once belonged to the German Luftwaffe. The Roosevelt and Andrews barracks were old brick structures, located in the southwestern part of Berlin.

Lieutenant Schwarzkopf received several promotions. When he first arrived, as platoon leader, he was responsible for a combat unit, Company D, in a brigade. They had to be properly trained and ready for combat. Next, he became liaison officer between his company and headquarters. Then, as a reconnaissance platoon leader, Norman was the eyes of the command for defending the American zone in case the Russians invaded areas outside East Berlin.

His final promotion during his second year in Berlin was as aide-de-camp to the commanding general, Brigadier General Charles Johnson. Acting as the general's right-hand man, Norman coordinated and scheduled General Johnson's daily activities. The position of aide was that of a diplomatic spokesman and alter ego for the general. The aide had to be reliable, hardworking, and have flawless judgment. To be selected was an honor.

Norman was living in a cosmopolitan city where he could enjoy German opera and music. He had a sports car and a large German shepherd named Troll. The dog and the lieutenant were often seen driving through the streets of Berlin.

Kenneth Leuer, a colleague from Fort Benning, was stationed in Mainz, Germany, near Frankfurt. Norman and Ken were assigned to a six-week training course at Oberammergau, a village in southwest Germany. On the weekends, the two men drove in Norman's sports car over the mountains to go skiing. After dinner at the Casa Cari-occa, they went to an ice show and met some of the skaters. Schwarzkopf and Leuer made frequent trips to see the shows and meet the skaters.

By July of 1961, First Lieutenant Schwarzkopf had become Captain Schwarzkopf. Soon he returned to the United States with his dog and went back to Fort Benning to take the infantry officer advanced course. For the year he was there, he shared a house off the post with two other men. This time, he and Troll rode around in a convertible.

Classes were held in Building 34. Students were given detailed instruction on air-land battle doctrine and how to coordinate air forces with ground forces. The lectures were intense, with breaks for coffee in the morning and afternoon. Leroy Suddath and Ken Leuer joined Norman for the course from 1961 to 1962. They formed a coffee-and-lunch group, which also included Bud Lawson and Zebb Bradford.

Leroy Suddath and Norman Schwarzkopf sat next to each other in their classes. "When we had to hand in our final paper, Norm sat in the back of the class, writing most of it through the whole period. The rest of us had struggled writing our

papers at home. He won the Marshall Award for
it," reminisced Leroy Suddath.

The title of that paper was "The Helmet." It
was a story about a general with a battered helmet,
who wins a battle against an enemy that has twice
as many troops. Exhausted, the general flashes back
to every move of the battle and reflects on what to
tell his commanders and staff at their meeting in
the war tent. He decides to explain how he used a
few fundamental principles of war to defeat the
enemy. As he places the smashed helmet back on
his head, the story ends.

"During that time, we would talk about what
makes a good general and who would be generals.
Norm had the ability to handle any situation. He
could talk to any class of people and on any subject. In conversation, he could move smoothly
from the man in the street to the queen of Eng-
land. He was a good decision man—quick, thor-
ough. He had presence and control. He could make
a dull incident sound exciting," remembered Ken
Leuer.

From the advanced course at Fort Benning,
Norman would go from Georgia to Los Angeles,
California, for a further two years as a student. The

army encouraged and paid for graduate studies for its career officers. Therefore, Captain Schwarzkopf devoted two years to obtaining a master of science degree in mechanical engineering at the University of Southern California. One classmate noted: "He was a brilliant person with a good sense of humor. He worked hard and played hard. In fact, he perfected his tennis game under the steady California sun."

That masters degree brought the 30-year-old Norman a professorship at his beloved West Point in 1964. He became an instructor in the Department of Mechanics. Back in the isolation of the academy grounds, Norman lived in the Bachelor Quarters, wedged against the steep cliff, overlooking the Hudson River.

Terry Hand, a one-time student of Captain Schwarzkopf, had vivid memories of the classroom in Bartlett Hall with its lattice windows and rows of tables. "Schwarzkopf taught a fundamental course in mechanics for cadets. Statics was the study of forces on bodies at rest. Dynamics was the study of the geometry of motion—orbits, rock tumbling, et cetera. He probably taught two hours a day, six days a week. He was big, burly, and loud—

like an actor. He used performing as a teaching technique. Because he was entertaining, it was interesting. He interacted with the class—eyeball to eyeball, and he could shame a student good-naturedly. His colleagues respected him but thought he was a wild and crazy guy," said Hand.

Events in Southeast Asia would influence Norman Schwarzkopf's future career choices. His original assignment to West Point was for three consecutive years. After the first year, he persuaded the authorities to put his other two teaching years on hold.

Chapter / Six

After Vietnam, Romance

Vietnam.

This small Southeast Asian country stretches along the Gulf of Tonkin and the South China Sea. The war that was waged there from 1961 to 1975 caused great anguish to the American people and its soldiers. Although many Americans supported the war in the beginning, they agonized over it the longer it lasted.

North and South Vietnam were divided. South Vietnam had become a republic in 1956. North Vietnam had turned to socialism and eventually communism because of the influence of the National Liberation Front, called the Vietcong. Despite South Vietnam's democratic aspirations, it was ruled first by a dynasty and then by strong military leaders. Intending to make all of Vietnam one republic under Communist rule, the North Vietnamese were sending guerrilla troops into South Vietnam for that purpose. The South Vietnamese government appealed to President John F. Kennedy in 1961 for assistance in maintaining freedom. He agreed to send military advisers to the South Vietnamese army.

In 1964, with the backing of Congress, President Lyndon B. Johnson signed the Gulf of Tonkin Resolution, which allowed American troops to fight alongside the South Vietnamese. The numbers of American troops would escalate after 1964 to more than 500,000.

When America's role became an active one in South Vietnam, Captain Norman Schwarzkopf was a restless observer on the West Point campus. Since he had been trained to defend the rights of freedom, he could not stand by without doing something. Therefore, he volunteered to serve in South Vietnam to protect the South Vietnamese people from being swallowed up by the Communist regime in North Vietnam.

Although Norman's two sisters were opposed to his participation in the war, he felt excitement and intense commitment as an airborne task force adviser to a South Vietnamese unit.

For a big, burly man like the young Captain Schwarzkopf, the steamy jungles of Vietnam were especially trying. In his role as adviser, Norman could have stayed behind the lines in more comfortable surroundings. But he chose to be in the front line with the South Vietnamese, where he ate, slept, and fought alongside them.

The Vietcong (guerrilla fighters) were a constant threat. Peasants in their traditional black clothing—men, women, and even children—who were working in the rice fields could lift a hoe that was really a rifle. Poison-tipped punji sticks could cause death if an unsuspecting soldier stepped on them in the watery rice paddies.

During those summer months of 1965, Schwarzkopf faced ambushes and the threat of death every day in the mountains near Cambodia. Three days before receiving his promotion to major, Schwarzkopf refused to follow an order from the South Vietnamese headquarters to take his troops into battle. Schwarzkopf discovered that his men didn't have enough fire and air support to protect them. This would have meant certain death.

Any battle operation required adequate cover. Four hours later, a panel of colonels sharply criticized him.

Norman's response was respectful but firm. "You're talking human lives," the captain told them, "and my responsibility is to accomplish the objective with a minimum loss of the troops under my command. That's my job—not just accomplishing the mission." Despite the outburst, Norman received his promotion to major.

Low-flying helicopters, painted dark camouflage green, were the only means of getting around quickly in Vietnam. Both sides of the helicopters were open so that troops could jump or roll out easily and the wounded to be loaded quickly. The helicopters would land and take off with barely a pause.

Once, when Major Schwarzkopf was surveying the situation of his troops from the air at Duc Co, he saw the results of an ambush and made the helicopter pilot land. He jumped out and helped stack the dead bodies of paratroopers and carry the wounded to the helicopters. At that time, Peter Arnett, who later reported from Baghdad for CNN during the 1991 Gulf War, was a reporter for the

Norman sits at the breakfast table with his nephew and niece in 1966. Norman's first tour in Vietnam changed him into a very serious young man.

Associated Press. He took a now famous photograph of Major Norman Schwarzkopf and a Vietnamese soldier supporting a wounded Vietnamese paratrooper between them.

On Valentine's Day, 1966, Major Schwarzkopf sustained four bullet wounds on the battlefield but refused to be treated until all his men were cared for. For this and other acts of valor, Schwarzkopf

was awarded two Silver Stars and two Purple
Hearts during his first tour in Vietnam.

West Point recalled Norman to finish his two-
year teaching contract. This time, he would be an
associate professor. The reception to the war in the
United States was not positive. There were antiwar
demonstrations in the streets of Washington, D.C.
College campuses were disrupted by students
protesting America's presence in Vietnam. Young
men were burning their draft cards and avoiding
confrontation by taking refuge in Canada.
Schwarzkopf, who supported America's presence in
Vietnam and his own duties there, was disillu-
sioned by the attitudes of the war protestors.

When Sally Schwarzkopf saw her brother after
his year in Vietnam, she noticed a change in him.
"After his first tour, he lost his youth when he
came back. . . . [H]e was just a very serious young
man," she said.

Only to the staff and cadets at West Point was
Schwarzkopf a hero. He had discharged his duties
courageously, honoring once more the West Point
motto: Duty, Honor, Country. But even some
young cadets were unwilling to leave the security of
West Point without putting on long-haired wigs to

avoid public anger. Students from Vassar College, protesting the war, placed daisies in the barrels of cadet rifles.

By the fall of 1967, Major Schwarzkopf was 33 years old and still unmarried. Then, on a football weekend, he met a young woman at the officers' club. A Trans World Airlines flight attendant based in New York, her name was Brenda Holsinger, from Timberville, Virginia. Two friends of hers had suggested she go with them for the weekend. The three stayed with Anthony and Mary Lou Bullotta on the grounds of West Point. Mary Lou remembered Brenda as "very petite and with the prettiest shoes." Tony Bullotta was the one who first introduced Norman and Brenda.

Within two months, Norman and Brenda became engaged. On July 6, 1968, the couple exchanged wedding vows in the famous Cadet Chapel at West Point.

After a brief honeymoon in Jamaica, the newlyweds were assigned to the Command and General Staff College at Fort Leavenworth, Kansas, for ten months. Major Schwarzkopf was promoted to lieutenant colonel before arriving. The Schwarzkopfs began married life under Kansas skies.

The wedding of Brenda and Norman at the West Point chapel in the summer of 1968

Set above the rolling plains, Fort Leavenworth is the oldest fort west of the Mississippi River. In 1827, fur traders unloaded their wagons on the banks of the Missouri River and rode past the fort on the Santa Fe and Oregon trails to sell their goods. The Native Americans were angry with these traders for trespassing on their land and so attacked them. The army post was established to protect the traders from the Native Americans. A maximum security military prison also was built here in 1875 to house 1,450 offenders. The famous Leavenworth federal penitentiary with its menacing guard tower is less than a mile from the fort.

At one time, Generals MacArthur and Eisenhower studied at this historic place. Lieutenant Colonel Schwarzkopf's name would be added to the list of notables 22 years later. The college is the army's senior school and teaches leaders how to train their units in the tactical and operational levels of war.

When Schwarzkopf completed his studies, he felt well informed on tactical warfare and volunteered to return to South Vietnam for a second tour. His bride realized that marriage to a military man would mean many moves. It also meant that her husband would face the dangers of war. Together they left Fort Leavenworth, Kansas. When Norman went to Vietnam, Brenda resumed her career with TWA.

To Schwarzkopf, the situation in Vietnam had worsened. The morale of the troops was at its lowest. High-ranking officers lived in comfortable homes with servants near the capital, Saigon, where they were far removed from the agony of

vicious warfare and the stench of death. "Careless-
ness, negligence, lousy leadership, and self-serving
officers and generals . . . who are more concerned
with their ambition than their troops . . . cost
human lives," said the lieutenant colonel.

After five months as executive officer to the
chief of staff in Saigon, he became commander of
the 1st Battalion, 6th Infantry of the 198th
Infantry Brigade, 23rd Infantry Division. At last,
he would be back in combat with his troops. Before
exchanging desk duties for live combat, he met
Brenda in Hong Kong for a brief vacation.

Once Norman moved to Chu Lai, near its airfield of sand-filled rice paddies, he tightened the
slipshod discipline of his battalion. He insisted that
the men wear their flak jackets despite the unbear-
able heat. He wouldn't let them ride on the tanks,
going through minefields and exposing themselves
as targets. Under their breath, some of his troops
called him Colonel Nazi.

From his helicopter, he saw a stranded patrol
trapped in a minefield. After landing, Schwarzkopf
tried to guide the men out of the minefield. One
soldier stepped on a mine and was blasted high in
the air, shattering an arm and a leg. Terrified, he

called for help. Schwarzkopf made his way carefully into the minefield. His knees were shaking so badly he had to lock his hands over them. Captain Bob Trabbert and three other soldiers stayed behind and watched. Upon reaching the frightened soldier, Schwarzkopf lowered his body on top of the young man to stop him from shaking. He asked Trabbert's men to cut some limbs from a nearby tree for splints. Another mine was set off accidentally, killing two other soldiers and dismembering Trabbert, who survived. Schwarzkopf was awarded his third Silver Star for saving the soldier.

During his two tours in Vietnam, Schwarzkopf's legendary temper was unleashed. On one occasion, he was radioing for helicopters to evacuate the wounded. The pilots rejected his request because they were transporting important officers in the area. With a blast of unbridled anger, he shouted over the airwaves that the lives of wounded soldiers were much more important. A helicopter responded immediately.

Another incident haunted him for many years. A company in his battalion was firing explosives at an enemy ridge when a howitzer shell fell short and killed a group of Americans. One of them was

Sergeant Michael E. Mullen from Iowa. The parents of this young man blamed Lieutenant Colonel Schwarzkopf for their son's death. Years later, a book, called *Friendly Fire*, was written by C. D. B. Bryan about this case. A television movie was made from it, too. Schwarzkopf denied the accusations from the Mullens and said, "I don't think it was an error of deliberate negligence."

Before Norman left Vietnam in 1970, he traveled to each one of his companies in the jungle to say his good-byes and thank-yous to the men who had served under him. In July, Schwarzkopf returned to Brenda and their new daughter, Cynthia.

Chapter / Seven

Crisscrossing the Country

Returning to America from Vietnam after his second tour was an even greater shock for Schwarzkopf. The antiwar movement had intensified. To further irritate his raw feelings, both his sisters were actively opposed to the Vietnam War.

Schwarzkopf was given a desk job at the Pentagon—his least favorite assignment. But he was back with Brenda. They took a small apartment in Annandale, Virginia. Although he disliked the battlefield of paperwork and politics, his family was a great comfort to him.

The Pentagon is a five-sided building with a hole in the center. Much of the surrounding 583 acres is devoted to parking lots. Set back from the narrow channel of the Potomac River, the flat-roofed structure, built in 1942, is opposite the Washington Monument. It contains the Department of Defense. The Pentagon employs 24,000 people, both civilian and military. Behind its sandy walls and columns are the headquarters for all the armed forces: army, navy, air force, marines, and Coast Guard. The chairman of the Joint Chiefs of Staff governs this nerve center of national defense from his wood-paneled office on the second floor.

Lining each of the six corridors, which run a total of 17.5 miles, are exhibits of flags and portraits of famous generals such as Eisenhower, Bradley, and Marshall. On each floor, the room numbers are coded for easy location. Getting lost in the myriad halls of the 29 acres inside the Pentagon is not difficult. However, those familiar with the shortcuts can get anywhere in the building in five minutes.

The Pentagon is like a city within a city. In the basement are banks, boutiques, fast-food restaurants, travel agencies, pharmacies, bookstores, and a terminal for the metro system. Here, too, are the Pentagon reporters next to the army operations center where all crises are handled. Just outside the structure is the Pentagon Officers' Athletic Club

An aerial view of the citylike Pentagon that houses the Department of Defense and employs 24,000 people

(POAC). In the center of the Pentagon are gazebos and landscaped picnic areas.

Lieutenant Colonel Schwarzkopf began the first of his four Pentagon assignments. This one, from 1970 to 1972, was in the Office of Personnel Operations. He was officer personnel directorate for the Infantry Branch. In essence, his responsibility was to prepare the paperwork for career changes of 40,000 army officers.

However, in November of 1970, Norman checked into the Walter Reed Hospital in Washington, D.C., for back surgery. His football injuries as a young man, irritated by parachute jumping in Vietnam, had left him in great pain. For months, Schwarzkopf lay still in a body cast while his back was mending. He spent long hours thinking and talking with fellow soldiers about the pros and cons of the Vietnam War. His wife and daughter visited him often to lift his spirits.

When he had recovered, he returned to the Pentagon. In the spring of 1972, his second daughter, Jessica, was born, adding to the family's joy.

An episode over dinner almost caused a permanent rift between Norman and his sister Sally. A television program about Vietnam provoked an emotional argument between them. He ordered her out of his house. The next morning, he called Sally to apologize. Both were in tears. After that incident, Schwarzkopf began to regard Vietnam more objectively.

Before long, the United States Army War Col-

lege in Carlisle, Pennsylvania, invited Schwarzkopf
to come for a ten-month intensive study program
for senior officers headed for key leadership roles in
the army. Since only 6 percent of colonels were
selected, this was an honor and a welcome change
for the Schwarzkopfs.

In the 1700s, Carlisle was used as a military
reservation to repel Native Americans and eventually to fight the British during the revolutionary
war. By 1900, Secretary of War Elihu Root thought
a war college was necessary. It was first located in
Washington, D.C., then moved to Fort Leavenworth, and in 1951 ended up in Carlisle.

Within the tight cluster of brick buildings and
barracks, Brenda, Norman, and their two daughters
would spend a happy year away from the Pentagon
and the Vietnam controversy. The aim of the college was to develop leaders with broad vision, one
not limited to just the military world. The purpose
was to encompass political and international
affairs. Norman joined almost 250 other students
in a six-course curriculum of military and international studies with a variety of electives. There
were small seminars in Root Hall and large lectures
in Bliss Hall. Each student was required to write a

two-hundred page paper at the year's end. Schwarzkopf's paper was titled "Military Merit: How to
Measure Who Measures Up."

Soon the academic year was over and Lieutenant Colonel Schwarzkopf tackled the unwel-
come duty of another Pentagon assignment from
1973 to 1974. This time, he worked in the Office
of the Assistant Secretary of the Army for Financial Management.

According to Charles A. Chase, who worked
with Schwarzkopf at that time: "We were in one of
the inside offices without windows, but there
wasn't time to worry about claustrophobia. We
were too busy. Although Norm had never worked
in financial management before, he picked it up
immediately. He worked on POM [Program of
Objective Management] to project the needs of the
military for the next five years. He had a brilliant
mind. Like many military officers, he didn't like
desk assignments, but he threw himself into whatever he had to do. The Pentagon is not the real
world for a military man, and dealing with Congress can be frustrating. On the battlefield or at
military posts, Norman Schwarzkopf competed and
dealt with problems that were real to him—train-

ing and instructing soldiers. But they don't come any more honest than Norman."

Unhappy to be confined again at the Pentagon, Schwarzkopf was delighted when he was offered a post no one else wanted—in Alaska. To be deputy commander, from 1974 to 1976, of the 172nd Infantry Brigade at Fort Richardson was an opportunity to leave behind both Washington, D.C., and the memories of Vietnam.

Alaska had been admitted in 1959 as the 49th state. For the Schwarzkopfs, it became a favorite appointment. The spectacular beauty and freedom of the outdoors were a happy change. Located northeast of the city of Anchorage, Fort Richardson sprawls over 62,000 acres in the foothills of the Chugach Mountains, which stretch 300 miles at a height of 8,000 feet.

Lieutenant Colonel Schwarzkopf's office was a spartan corner room in a wing of Building 1. His wooden desk was at an angle and his walls were bare. Only a leather chair and couch filled the rest of the space. Two enlisted soldiers sat outside his office. One was his driver, and the other was an administrative clerk.

Schwarzkopf trained his men hard. Because of

the soft tundra in summer and generally icy roads in winter, tanks and heavy vehicles would sink or slide and therefore couldn't be used. Airplanes and snowmobiles were the means of transportation.

In August 1975, Norman Schwarzkopf organized a march that no participant would ever forget. On a highway beyond Fort Richardson, Schwarzkopf led 2,500 infantrymen 75 miles northward to Talkeetna. They marched for three days, Schwarzkopf sleeping close by his soldiers. On tables alongside the road were food and water to grab and eat. The men groaned from sore muscles and blistered feet. Here, Norman earned his nickname Bear—sometimes "grizzly" and sometimes "teddy." At some point, the tag of Stormin' Norman was attached to him, too. He preferred the nickname Bear.

Reaching their destination was only the beginning of this military exercise, called the Ace Card of Chulitna. They had to wage a mock battle through rugged mountain passes, and outwit the enemy, played by troops from Fort Wainwright. Schwarzkopf and his men won. "He could read your mind and heartbeat," said one of his aides. By November 1975, Norman Schwarzkopf was awarded a promotion to full colonel.

Deputy Commander Schwarzkopf leads a 3-day, 75-mile march in Alaska.

Struck by the breadth and beauty of Alaska, Norman wanted his sister Sally to see this vast land. When she came, the whole family squeezed into a camper and drove 250 miles north to McKinley National Park (now called Denali National Park) to see the wildlife, the hills of black and white spruce, the valleys, and the glacial streams. Brother and sister fished for salmon and trout and viewed the white splendor of Mount McKinley.

An expedition the colonel made alone was a weekend trek along the ridge of the speckled green mountains, extending from Cook Inlet to the Seward Peninsula. After Schwarzkopf hiked over Resurrection Pass Trail for 38 miles, his wife, Brenda, picked him up. Schwarzkopf's feet were bleeding from the rough and rocky terrain he had traveled, but his grin expressed his pleasure with the accomplishment.

Sad to leave the rugged wilderness, Colonel Schwarzkopf was somewhat pacified by his transfer to Fort Lewis, 50 miles south of Seattle, Washington—not that far from Alaska. At this post, Norman became the commander of the First Brigade of the Ninth Division. A brigade is a portion of a division, and Schwarzkopf had charge of more than 1,500 men.

Although not as dramatic as Alaska, Fort Lewis was surrounded by beauty. On clear days, Mount Rainier could be seen in the distance. Gentle rains and veils of fog were part of the weather scene much of the year.

During one of Colonel Schwarzkopf's training maneuvers under the direction of General Richard E. Cavazos, his men made some glaring mistakes—such as positioning artillery to face the wrong direction. Before Cavazos could give Schwarzkopf a negative critique, the colonel admitted the mistake and asked the general to let his men try again in six weeks. Cavazos recognized Schwarzkopf's admission of failure as a real sign of leadership. The two men became great friends.

The year 1976 brought both sadness and joy to Norman Schwarzkopf. His mother, who had moved from East Orange, New Jersey, to live with her daughter, Sally, in Bethesda, Maryland, died. She was buried at West Point alongside her husband. Her death brought the Schwarzkopf sisters and brother closer once again. Later that year, to Norman and Brenda's pure delight, she gave birth to a son, Christian, named after Norman's great-grand-father.

The Schwarzkopfs were sad to leave Fort Lewis in July 1978. However, the newest posting for the Schwarzkopfs had a romantic ring to it—Hawaii. Although Norman was not in charge of soldiers, he traveled extensively in the Far East. At Camp Smith, which is on a ridge west of Honolulu, he became deputy director for plans in the Pacific Command. Essentially, the navy had command of the Pacific theater of operations from there. The other military services—army, marines, and air force—worked together. Schwarzkopf was responsible for coordinating contingency and exercise plans in the event of a war threat. The surprise attack on Pearl Harbor naval base in 1941 would not be repeated.

Shortly after his arrival, H. Norman Schwarzkopf was promoted to brigadier general, earning his first star as a general. Though not a challenging post, the experience of traveling and coordinating the services would prove useful during the Gulf War.

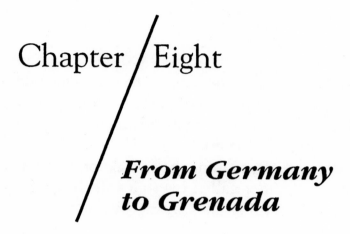

Chapter / Eight

From Germany to Grenada

The posting in Hawaii was over in 1980 for the Schwarzkopf family. The military authorities ordered them across the Atlantic to the banks of the Rhine River, where they made their new home in Mainz, Germany.

Mainz is a major city, bordering Wiesbaden and not far from Frankfurt. Heavily bombed during World War II because of its strategic location on the Rhine, Mainz has historic as well as military importance.

Brigadier General H. Norman Schwarzkopf became the assistant division commander of the Eighth Infantry Division (mechanized). The head-quarters was in an old cavalry area, and the bar-racks were right in the middle of the city. Lee Bar-

racks had the highest density of troops, squeezed
into pre-World War I facilities. Because tanks
moved noisily and constantly through the main
streets, many citizens complained. According to
one officer who served under Schwarzkopf, the new
division commander called his staff into his office
and said: "If anything goes wrong in the commu-
nity, you have failed your job."

There was another problem Schwarzkopf
inherited. Drug and alcohol abuse was rampant
among the soldiers, putting Mainz on the chart as
the number two offender in Europe. Schwarzkopf
made it clear to his officers that he wanted that
problem solved. To cure the boredom, clubs and
activities were organized to keep the men occupied.

Along with these problems, there was the
spread of terrorism throughout Europe. Norman's
classmate from West Point, General James L.
Dozier, posted in Italy, was kidnapped by terrorists.
Fortunately he was rescued, but Norman became
very cautious about preventing any possible terror-
ist attacks in Mainz. Iron bars were put on the
headquarters buildings. He posted troops at either
end of the street where he and his family lived.
Daily, his office was searched for bombs, and he

picked up his son every day after school to make sure he was safe.

Another unexpected military expense occurred during the pope's visit to Mainz in November 1980. The mayor of Mainz approached Schwarzkopf to see if the military airfield could be used to accommodate the pope's visit and if the brigadier general would act as host. Schwarzkopf agreed. He saw this as an opportunity to raise funds to build a skeet range for his troops and officers. Authorizing the purchase of 100,000 ham-and-cheese sandwiches at one dollar each, Schwarzkopf expected to make a hefty profit at the concession stands.

Unfortunately, the day of the pope's appearance at the airfield was gray and dismal. The German people did not turn out in the thousands. Only 2,000 sandwiches were sold. Left with 98,000 sandwiches, Schwarzkopf relieved a lieutenant colonel of all his other duties and ordered him to sell the sandwiches. By the time they numbered 42,000, most of the sandwiches had freezer burn and had to be destroyed. Many of Schwarzkopf's colleagues teased him about this ham-and-cheese failure.

Two years passed before Schwarzkopf was reas-

signed. Then, Brenda packed the family belongings
for their return to Washington, D.C. Before they
left, Schwarzkopf was promoted to major general.
This time, his Pentagon assignment would be for
less than a year as director of military personnel
management, in the Office of the Deputy Chief of
Staff for Personnel. Colonel Mo Faber remembered
that Schwarzkopf "let you know where you stood.
He was a decisive individual."

In June 1983, the Schwarzkopfs were delighted
with their new posting to Fort Stewart, Georgia.
Here, Norman could hunt and fish while being the
commanding general of the 24th Infantry Division
(mechanized) with its heavy tanks and artillery.

The family exchanged the sticky summers of
Virginia for the steamy swamps and forests of Georgia. At Fort Stewart, Major General Schwarzkopf
trained his troops and tanks five days a week and
insisted the men spend the weekends with their
families.

The commanding general's residence at Fort
Stewart is a comfortable one-story ranch on a circle
near the golf course. The raising and lowering of
the flag at sunrise and sunset are daily rituals,
accompanied by the firing of a howitzer, which can

be heard throughout much of the post. Wherever any military personnel are at that moment, they must stop what they're doing and stand at attention. An MP (military police) can issue a ticket to anyone not showing proper respect for the flag. During the lowering of the flag one afternoon, Schwarzkopf looked out his window at the golf course and saw some of his men continuing to play without a moment's pause for respect. Next morning from his corner office on the second floor of headquarters, he telephoned the golf course. "When the flag is raised or lowered on my post, everyone will acknowledge it or I'll bring my . . . tanks over to your golf course and you won't have a golf course!" he said.

Fort Stewart is a prestigious post, which dates back to the revolutionary war. It was used more recently in the Vietnam and Persian Gulf wars. The commanding general makes sure the soldiers are trained and ready for deployment. The post's easy access to the seaports of Savannah, Georgia, and Charleston, South Carolina, make it a strategic location.

For Schwarzkopf, the Georgia forests and ponds were ideal for hunting deer, quail, dove, and

Norman with his black Labrador, Bear

turkey. He befriended the game warden for Fort Stewart, Odis W. King, and together they went bass fishing. Metts Pond, with its 17 acres of snags, logs, and trees, was Norman's favorite. From a rowboat, King taught the commander how to fish for bass with surface bait. Brenda frequently called upon Mrs. King for instructions on cooking the wild game Norman brought home.

According to the game warden: "Norman Schwarzkopf didn't want anything from me and never asked anything. He told me he had to watch those who were trying to butter him up. He loved his family. When his daughter was a cheerleader, he was there for her first night."

After one of those successful fishing expeditions on a Sunday in October 1983, Norman came home to cook the bass for his family. He had already made the cornmeal batter when the telephone rang; he was asked to go on a secret mission for several weeks. Before he could cook or serve his family the bass, he was on a plane heading for Norfolk, Virginia. No one knew where he was going—not even Brenda. Norman guessed (wrongly) that it would be Beirut, Lebanon. Brenda gave the fish to Norman's personal aide, Dennis Grice, to share with his family.

That same Sunday, President Ronald Reagan and Secretary of State George Shultz were in Augusta, Georgia, playing golf. They were called from Washington about the threat of a Communist takeover on the small island of Grenada in the West Indies. There were 400 medical students from the United States at the American university there, who might be in danger. Vice President George Bush asked for the president's permission to stage an invasion to evacuate the students and free the Grenadians. Reagan gave Bush the go-ahead.

Norman Schwarzkopf's name had been suggested for this duty by his old friend General Richard E. Cavazos, who was now at Fort Mac-Pherson, Georgia. Essentially, this would be a naval operation with marines and army as ground forces. The navy needed an adviser for these ground troops, and Cavazos said Schwarzkopf was their man. The navy was not very happy about having an army general working alongside it in what would be called Operation Urgent Fury. However, Schwarzkopf convinced the admiral that he was only interested in a successful outcome and in working together with him.

Grenada is a small, mountainous island with white sandy beaches and pastel-colored homes. It is only 12 miles wide and 21 miles long. The population at that time was under 100,000. Christopher Columbus had sighted the island in 1498. Eventually, Grenada came under British rule until it became independent in 1974. Then, in 1979, a Socialist named Maurice Bishop conducted a bloodless coup to overthrow Sir Eric Gairy as prime minister.

Once Bishop became prime minister, he established ties with Cuba and the Soviet Union, much

Under General Schwarzkopf's command, helicopters rescued 400 medical students from Grenada.

to the displeasure of the United States. When a 9,500-yard airstrip began to be constructed by Cubans, some residents became suspicious. Patricia White, an American resident, heard goods being unloaded from ships in the dark at three and four in the morning on the weekends. White followed the trucks in her car. They went to the new airfield and unloaded weaponry and rockets. But despite her repeated eyewitness testimony to the State Department, White was not believed.

After the invasion of Grenada, it was discovered that the Soviets had intended to establish a base there and to mount antiaircraft missiles. An East German reporter for *Le Monde*, a French newspaper, recognized the weaponry from the shape of the buildings he had seen the Russians use in East Germany.

Since the United States intelligence had come from British sources, the information about subversive activities was considered secondhand. However, Eugenia Charles, prime minister of Dominica, had been the one to warn President Reagan earlier about the Cuban and Russian threat. Other Caribbean states met in Barbados, recommending American intervention.

Schwarzkopf found himself on the naval aircraft carrier USS *Guam*, which plowed through the sea to reach the outer coast of Grenada to be at the center of Operation Urgent Fury.

Meanwhile, Bishop had been taken under house arrest on October 19, 1983, after a Communist coup by his deputy, Edward Coard. Bishop was murdered shortly after his capture.

These events led to American intervention. Except for a few early naval failures to land commando units on the island, General Schwarzkopf, as deputy commander of the task force, helped to organize the landings of the marines and paratroopers. One young officer, Oliver North, was in charge of the marines. The military insisted on a blackout of the press, which brought an outcry of protest when the completed operation was revealed.

The medical students were rescued and evacuated by helicopter to the *Guam*. Marines and paratroopers stormed the new airstrip and fought Cubans and Russians until they surrendered. When Schwarzkopf flew onto the island to inspect, he saw from the air a wall on which was scrawled GOD BLESS AMERICA.

Because of damage from the invasion, Grenada needed to repair broken water mains, sewers, electricity wiring, and telephone lines. Ted Morse, from USAID in Barbados, was sent over to fix them, and to oversee the safety of the American students. When Morse met Schwarzkopf on the island, Schwarzkopf said to him, "Look, I've got men and no money, and you've got money and no men, so we'll marry them up and they're all yours." Morse said that the military men pitched in to renovate schools and repair all the civilian needs. He commended Schwarzkopf for his breadth of understanding.

When Schwarzkopf returned to Fort Stewart, his welcome was that of a hero—quite different from his reception when he returned from Vietnam. He spoke at one of the elementary schools on the post and told the children about the Grenada experience. At the end, he said to them, "Appreciate your parents. Your mothers and fathers are gone a lot in the military, but you should understand they are doing their jobs. You should be proud of them."

The day of departure from Fort Stewart was not an easy one for Norman Schwarzkopf and his family. They had been happy there and had made many good friends. Jane Tutten, his secretary there, would miss seeing Schwarzkopf's black Labrador retriever, Bear, and the children, who often came up the back stairs to his office. On that final day, when Schwarzkopf was alone in his office before the change of command ceremony, Tutten heard her boss crying quietly. She didn't intrude because she knew that she would cry, too.

Chapter / Nine

Promotions to the Best Posts

Perhaps those tears in Georgia were caused by a mixture of sorrow and disappointment at going back to the Pentagon. Major General Schwarzkopf knew that he would be confined indoors to office work. However, this appointment to become assistant deputy chief of staff for operations and plans (ADCSOPS) was seen as the beginning of a series of choice assignments in the army structure. Schwarzkopf would be in the halls of the Pentagon from July 1985 to June 1986. His job was to be an adviser and alternate to the deputy chief of staff.

Schwarzkopf's office was to the left of a central area for the two secretaries and two officers. The deputy's office was to the right. Their windows overlooked Arlington National Cemetery, which was a constant reminder of the price of war—human lives.

His secretary said: "He was a good boss with a lot of humor. This was a busy job and an important job. He had to know what was going on in the world. He was constantly going up to the Joint Chiefs of Staff for briefings. He could become upset, but he got over it right away."

The year passed quickly, and Norman Schwarzkopf was promoted to lieutenant general. His new orders took him back to Fort Lewis in Washington State. As commanding general of I Corps, he couldn't have been happier. His family lived in a stately two-story residence that looked down Watkins Field to Mount Rainier.

From the summer of 1986 to the summer of 1987, the Schwarzkopfs enjoyed outdoor life. Every Wednesday at lunchtime, Schwarzkopf could be found at the skeet range on the post. Norman Neubert, who was in charge of the range, joked with the general and noted that he never pulled rank. Schwarzkopf began teaching his son, Christian, at the age of eleven or twelve how to shoot skeet with a rifle and aim at the clay disks meant to represent moving birds. "The general loved to hunt pheas-

Norman practices one of his favorite pastimes, skeet shooting.

ant, duck, grouse, and chucker. On vacation, he went trout fishing in the Columbia River," said Neubert.

"He would talk to anyone, anywhere, anytime. Officers like to talk to low-ranking people to find out what's going on," said Neubert. "His philosophy was to do your job and do it to the best of your ability. If you do it wrong, you'll hear from him."

According to British-born Kenneth Greenwood, who was stationed at Fort Lewis: "If the helicopters were not on time, he was snarly. He was death on majors and colonels and captains. But he was fatherly to first and second lieutenants. He was listened to by sergeants and noncommissioned officers. He was a soldier's soldier."

Often, there would be a division run at 5:00 A.M., and 10,000 feet could be heard clumping on Gray's Airfield. On Law Day, May 1, 1987, General Schwarzkopf demanded that the whole corps appear on the parade field before dawn. It was pitch-black. The men groaned.

With a searchlight shining on an American flag billowing in the breeze and held up with a crane, Schwarzkopf shouted into the microphone, "Are you proud to be an American?"

The corps answered in unison, "Yes." He asked them to raise their right hands and take the oath of allegiance.

"I declare the rest of the day a holiday, but first, please join me in singing 'God Bless America,' " said the general. Then fireworks sprayed the black, predawn skies.

Sometimes, the general had to give speeches to world affairs groups or local Rotarians as a matter of public relations. At such times, he could have fun with the press. Bob Rosenburgh, a designer of military vehicles and a public relations officer for General Schwarzkopf at Fort Lewis, remembered an incident with a number of journalists from Seattle. They asked him for the "real story" behind the Grenada invasion. Schwarzkopf pulled his tall frame up from his chair, crossed the room to close the door, and said he would tell them if none of it would be printed. They promised. He proceeded to tell them in detail the contingency plans for Grenada, but newspaper ethics prevented them from ever printing the information!

However, at the end of Schwarzkopf's tour at Fort Lewis, the post historian, Joe Huddleston, who plans a battle analysis twice a year, used the Grenada invasion as his subject. For three days, the military staff wrestled with this historic battle setting and determined what they would do under standard operating procedures. General Schwarzkopf role-played President Reagan. At the conclusion of the intellectual exercise, Schwarzkopf took four hours to show slides of the actual invasion and answered many questions.

Once again, the Pentagon had summoned the happy general to leave his post for the cement walls of the Defense Department in Washington,

D.C. From fall 1987 to October of 1988, Schwarzkopf would assume a very high-ranking position—
deputy chief of staff for operations and plans
(DCSOPS). He was back in the same office with
Millie and Margaret, his two secretaries. This time,
his office was on the right. Margaret said: "He
made things happen and was very fast on his feet.
When he was first appointed, he called the staff
into his office to warn them that if they heard of
anything illegal or shady going on, to come talk
with him. You knew where you stood with him. He
was smart and moved papers quickly and held people responsible. He had a dry humor, teasing and
cracking jokes."

The DCSOPS job is the army's nerve center
and is a diverse operation. It deals with national
policy on strategy formulation; that is, what kind of
army we should build and whether we should use
light or heavy infantry. Decisions to utilize nuclear
and chemical weapons are made here. As deputy
chief of staff, Schwarzkopf reported to the army
chief of staff on joint matters for all armed services
as well as on national security and military matters
relating to international affairs. In fact, DCSOPS

was almost like a think tank for the Joint Chiefs of Staff.

Colonel Faber recalled what it was like to be briefed by General Schwarzkopf after a meeting with the Joint Chiefs of Staff. "As he was coming back to the office, he would be on standby. Once he was in the door, he took out his notes and gave us the hot wash. This was an immediate debriefing of what happened. You could argue with him, but once the decision was made, you had to support it."

His friend Charles Chase remembered Schwarzkopf at DCSOPS as "flying out the mall entrance of the Pentagon to go to a Boy Scout meeting with his son and doing magic tricks for them." It seemed he was never too busy for his family.

On November 23, 1988, when Lieutenant General Schwarzkopf was promoted to four-star general at the Pentagon's Hall of Heroes, it was a very emotional moment for him. In accepting this honor, he expressed appreciation to his wife, Brenda.

After the ceremony, General Schwarzkopf's orders were to serve out his final three years before retirement at MacDill Air Force Base in Tampa,

In 1988 Norman Schwarzkopf was promoted to four-star general at the Pentagon's Hall of Heroes.

Florida. He would be the commander in chief of the United States Central Command, established in January 1983. There would be no troops for the general to command, but he would be supervising United States military activity and security in several countries from the Middle East to the Far East. These countries were Iran, Iraq, Kuwait, Saudi Arabia, Qatar, Somalia, United Arab Emirates, Yemen, Egypt, Bahrain, Djibouti, Jordan, Ethiopia, Kenya, Oman, Afghanistan, and Pakistan.

MacDill Air Force Base is a peninsula that juts out into Tampa Bay. Because MacDill is a training base, F-16s constantly shriek and slice across the skies. Conversations are drowned in their wake. Palm trees—tied with yellow ribbons during the Gulf War—line the way to the Central Command headquarters.

Inside the brown-trimmed, stucco building, some 800 to 900 people busily sift through daily intelligence information about the countries of their concern. General Schwarzkopf settled into the corner office. From the smoke-tinted windows, the four-star general could look out over Tampa Bay and see the flagpole planted firmly in the ground.

However, Schwarzkopf sat at his desk with his back to the bay. On his desk was a carved bear. On his walls were knives from the Middle East, some West Point mementos, and a large map displaying the areas of his responsibility. Alongside the map was a clock showing times throughout the world. His furniture was of leather and dark wood. Outside his office sat his aide, Colonel Burwell B. Bell, and the general's secretary, Mrs. Williams.

Not far from the office, the Schwarzkopfs moved into a spacious, Spanish-style residence, designated for the presiding commander. While in Tampa, Cindy and Jessica would finish high school and start college while Christian would pass some of his preteen and teen years. Brenda entered into base activities with the wives. Norman found time to fish and hunt with Christian and go hiking and kayaking with the girls. Their dog, Bear, was lovable, but poorly disciplined. He joined the fun whenever he was allowed.

Those working for Norman Schwarzkopf at Central Command learned that he meant business. His temper would flare at incompetence or sloppiness. For instance, according to the military network: "He was an information junkie. He wanted the early bird newspaper from the Pentagon on his desk at 7:30 A.M. sharp. If it was a minute late, heads would roll. The fax machine might have had difficulties, but that didn't matter to him."

When questioned about his temper, the general replied to a reporter: "I wish I wasn't so quick to anger. An awful lot has been written about my temper. I get angry at a principle, not a person. Anytime I get angry, I feel terrible about it afterward, and if ever I think I have devastated a human being because of my temper, I always make it a point to go back to them and apologize."

To familiarize himself with his area of responsibility (AOR), General Schwarzkopf traveled several times to the countries to meet the heads of state. Like his father before him, he was respectful of others' customs and cultures. In fact, during a trip to Kuwait in 1989, he was offered a traditional white flowing Arab robe to wear. After putting it on over his uniform, he looked at himself in the mirror and swung around in a circle. He felt quite comfortable in his Arab attire throughout the evening.

However, General Schwarzkopf did not feel comfortable about the mood in the Middle East.

He testified before Senate hearings that he felt Iraq
was a potentially troubled area. Iraq had waged an
eight-year war with its neighbor Iran, squabbling
over land and oil. Saddam Hussein, Iraq's leader,
had used chemical warfare to exterminate the
opposing armies of Iran. Hussein claimed to have
the fourth-largest army in the world and was
believed to have a potentially dangerous nuclear
weapons capacity.

Although the United States had friendly relations with Hussein and Iraq until 1990,
Schwarzkopf was uneasy about an Iraqi threat once
the eight-year war with Iran was over. Therefore, in
July of 1990, he and his staff made contingency
plans in case of war in the Middle East. They went
to North Florida to engage in a mock exercise
named Internal Look '90.

Only days after their return, a telephone call
came from General Colin L. Powell, chairman of
the Joint Chiefs of Staff in Washington, D.C. He
warned Schwarzkopf that the Iraqis were moving
their military tanks and 95,000 soldiers close to the
border of Kuwait.

Another telephone call came from Powell a

day or two later. "They've crossed over," said Powell on August 2, 1990.

Immediately, General Schwarzkopf flew to Washington, D.C., to consult with Secretary of Defense Dick Cheney and Colin Powell. The three of them met with President George Bush. Schwarzkopf explained in detail the exercise plan already in place. This plan would become known as Desert Shield, the military buildup in defense of Saudi Arabia from further aggression by Saddam Hussein of Iraq.

At first, Schwarzkopf and others thought the Iraqis were only interested in seizing the Kuwaiti oil fields and the two islands, Rumaila and Būbiyān, which would provide shipping access to the Persian Gulf. Apparently, Saddam Hussein also had a greedy eye on Saudi Arabia and its rich oil fields.

The next move was for Schwarzkopf and Cheney to go to Saudi Arabia to see its leader, King Fahd. Arabs spent many hours sipping coffee with him. This is the Arab way of getting acquainted with visitors and establishing mutual trust. Schwarzkopf had been groomed for this kind

of diplomacy. If the Saudis wanted military defense
of their country, the Americans and their allies
were prepared to do it. General H. Norman
Schwarzkopf embraced the king of Saudi Arabia as
had his father 40 years before. King Fahd was
impressed with the directness of the younger
Schwarzkopf and accepted President Bush's offer to
defend Saudi Arabia.

"We will come if asked and will leave when
asked," said the general, assuring the king of a limited military presence.

Arrangements were under way at Central
Command to assemble all forces to travel 10,000
miles to Saudi Arabia. Lieutenant General Charles
R. Horner, commander of the Air Force Command
for Central Command, conferred with General
Schwarzkopf and agreed to stay in Riyadh, Saudi
Arabia, while Schwarzkopf prepared and pushed
the forces to move to the Middle East.

Horner and Schwarzkopf had worked together
within Central Command. Schwarzkopf liked
Horner's honesty and outspokenness. He listened
to Horner's advice about air power. Of Schwarzkopf, Horner has said: "He is an extremely bright
man who knows his strengths and few weaknesses.

He should be remembered as a hero, for he was obsessed with keeping the loss of American lives to an absolute minimum."

From Fort Stewart, Georgia, the highways were jammed with M1A1 tanks, M2 Bradley vehicles, TOW vehicles, HMMWVs, and M102 105mm tow howitzers. The M1A1 tanks can sustain 12 hits and are air-conditioned. There were Chinook, Black-hawk, Cobra, and Apache helicopters, and jeeps (regular and special forces dune-buggy types for the navy SEALS), rolling to Savannah, Georgia. There, they were loaded on seven ships going to the Middle East. This was Schwarzkopf's memorable 24th Infantry (mechanized) joining Desert Shield. His old 101st Airborne Assault Division from Fort Campbell, Kentucky, was transported there, as was the 82nd Airborne from Fort Bragg, North Carolina. Naval ships and aircraft carriers soon were steaming to the Persian Gulf. Tough, trained marines loaded their equipment onto the ships, ready, along with naval air and sea support, for a beach attack on Kuwait.

Chapter / Ten

Commanding the Persian Gulf War

Schwarzkopf's job was to choreograph all the allied services under one command. In the latter part of August, he and his staff left behind the humidity of Florida for the windswept sands of Saudi Arabia. Before Schwarzkopf left, Lieutenant General John J. Yeosock, a 1955 graduate of Valley Forge Military Academy, in charge of the army portion of Central Command, sat down with Schwarzkopf and suggested taking the Patriot missile to the theater of operations. The technology on this weapon had been modified over a period of 20 years. During the Gulf War, Patriot missiles would save many lives by destroying the Scud missiles aimed at Saudi Arabia and Israel from Iraq.

Months after the Gulf War, a controversy

developed over the actual effectiveness of the Patriot missile. However, according to a historian at the Center of Military History in Washington, D.C., the Patriot, which looks like a giant cartridge, performed well in the Gulf War. The Patriot was built to intercept airplanes and missiles. When aimed at the single warhead of a Scud missile launched by the Iraqis, the Patriot intercepted and destroyed the Scud. Because the Iraqi Scuds were so poorly made, they splintered into pieces in the air. A Patriot would seek and destroy the largest piece of each Scud—not always the warhead. But Patriots destroyed 45 of the 47 Scuds fired.

The Middle East is composed of 22 countries from Morocco to Yemen and to the borders of Afghanistan and Pakistan. Many are home to ancient tribal societies. Although Iran is the largest country in the area, Iraq has a great variety of terrain for its size. It has rivers, mountains, desert, deltas, oil fields, and good crop lands. Many of its people are graduates of Iraqi universities. But the military rulers have wasted the country's natural resources since 1955. Saddam Hussein, appointed president and chairman of the Revolutionary Council in 1979, did the same by depleting the country's finances and supporting a large army in its eight-year-long war against Iran. He also built powerful chemical and nuclear reactor facilities.

Kuwait, on the other hand, is a tiny country with a total population of two million. Only 570,000 are Kuwaitis. The rest come from Palestine and Iraq. Many of those were evicted after the war. There are no mountains or natural water, but Kuwaitis have rich oil fields, capable of producing 70 billion barrels per year, and they trade all over the world. They also have spices, perfumes, and gold. Iraq wanted this small country to become its 19th province.

Saudi Arabia is one of Kuwait's neighbors. It is a big country, prospering from oil discoveries made 50 years ago. The Saudis are a gracious people— and not power hungry.

Riyadh, Saudi Arabia, is a modern city with many new buildings, shops, and a population of a million and a half. Its old brick buildings blend harmoniously with its modern architecture of tinted glass and sharp angles and lines. The Ministry of the Interior is like a round spaceship. Wide boulevards are lined with trees that are kept alive with pumped water. Saudi Arabia's oil wealth attracts many foreigners, corporations, and engineers.

For the duration of the Gulf War, the Saudis offered General Schwarzkopf any palatial residence he wished. Instead, he bunked in a tiny room near the War Room, four stories below ground in the Saudi Ministry of Defense and Aviation (MODA). The general slept only a few hours each night under his camouflage poncho bedspread. He listened to cassettes of opera singer Luciano Pavarotti and of the sounds of nature. A shotgun rested beside his bed. Photographs of his family, a Bible, and a book about Sherman's Civil War campaigns were at his bedside.

Sensitive to the religious customs of the Muslims in Saudi Arabia, General Schwarzkopf spoke for an hour to more than 800 chaplains from the United States armed services stationed in Saudi Arabia. According to one chaplain: "The general told us that the Saudi society was like a three-legged stool. One leg was for business, one for tribal customs, and one for Islam. Each was necessary for the society to remain intact. He indicated that King Fahd was concerned that the presence of U.S.

troops might convert some of his people to Christianity and corrupt Islamic society. So the general advised us to practice our religion in a discreet way, in order not to threaten or interfere with the Saudi culture and customs."

To prevent conflict and resentment from the Saudi people, no alcohol, drugs, or pornography were allowed. Nor were American women permitted outside the confines of the desert barracks unless their arms and legs were adequately covered.

While the American Secretary of State James A. Baker was trying to work out a diplomatic and peaceful outcome of the Iraqi invasion into Kuwait, General Schwarzkopf spent seven months building the troop force to 641,000 from the United States armed services. Some 241,000 were from the regular army, navy, marines, and air force. The other 200,000 were voluntary reservists. A further 200,000 were from coalition forces. To avoid boredom and possible morale problems in the desert, Schwarzkopf insisted that the troops train and rehearse every day. This also would ensure preparedness.

President and Mrs. Bush flew to Saudi Arabia in November and ate Thanksgiving dinner with

the troops located on the desert plains. Schwarzkopf also left his War Room to spend Christmas
with his troops, who were waiting to attack Iraq's
Republican Guards.

On August 2, 1990, the United Nations Security Council had passed Resolution 660. The resolution condemned Iraq for invading Kuwait and
stated that Iraq should withdraw unconditionally
from Kuwait. On November 29, 1990, the United
Nations passed another Resolution, 678, which set
a deadline of January 15, 1991, for the Iraqis to
withdraw completely from Kuwait. If they did not,
the United Nations authorized the United States
and member states to "use all necessary means"
against the Iraqis. Saddam Hussein rejected both
resolutions.

At midnight on January 16, 1991, Operation
Desert Shield became Operation Desert Storm.
General Schwarzkopf called the Central Command
chaplain, Colonel David Peterson, into the War
Room to offer a prayer before going into battle.
Schwarzkopf was pacing back and forth. "We are
sending a lot of people to their deaths," he said.

"I prayed that God would intervene and control
the weather on our behalf," said Colonel Peterson.

"We want to win this war with as few losses as possible," stated Schwarzkopf. He then played country singer Lee Greenwood's tune "God Bless the U.S.A." At 3:00 A.M. on January 17, Schwarzkopf gave Lieutenant General Horner the signal to begin the air phase of the war. His Saudi counterpart, Lieutenant General Khaled bin Sultan al-Saud, was also ready with his Saudi pilots.

The Saudi general later said of Norman Schwarzkopf: "We spent many days and nights together. War has a way of bonding military men in deep friendship." To graduates of Auburn University in Montgomery, Alabama, he said in December 1991, after receiving an honorary degree, "The West and Arabs marched together and shed their blood together. All nations worked together to destroy aggression. *Miracle* is not too strong a word. No one hates war more than those who are in it."

Throughout the Persian Gulf War, President Bush gave General Schwarzkopf the freedom to direct all campaigns and strategies without interference from the White House. This was a drastic change from the Vietnam War, when the generals in the field had had very little control over the mil-

General Schwarzkopf was first in line to greet the returning Prisoners of War as they arrived in Saudi Arabia.

itary objectives. General Schwarzkopf was definitely in control of all ground, sea, and air operations. The White House, together with the Defense Department, made only the decisions when to start and end the war.

On January 17, 1991, Lieutenant General Charles R. Horner instructed the allies from nine countries in the coalition air force to start the 2,000 air sorties a day against Iraq. They were intended to strike all military installations and to bomb bridges in order to cut off supplies to the Iraqi troops. Horner used an assortment of aircraft: F-117 Stealth bombers, F-15s (C and E models), F-16s, F-111s, EF-111s, AWACS, B-52s, C-5s, C-

141s, and C-130s. With typical modesty, General
Schwarzkopf gave credit to General Horner and
said: "The air war is Horner's baby."

To retaliate, beginning on the morning of January 18, the Iraqi invaders bombarded Saudi Arabia and Israel with Scud missiles. The United States hoped the Israelis would not return the Iraqi attack. This might have caused a larger war in the Middle East. The Israelis did not respond. Trained personnel from the United States operated the Patriots in Israel to intercept and destroy some of the Iraqi Scuds. A few Scuds fell into the ocean while others did cause damage in Israel.

From Riyadh to Baghdad, Iraq's capital, the January and February nights were haunted by the wailing sound of sirens and the bursting thump of bombs. Antiaircraft fire splintered the darkness with threads of light over Baghdad.

For the coalition forces, the 127-degree desert heat of August was past. Now the troops faced bitter cold, rainy nights, and swirling sandstorms. The cold was preferable to the heat for a ground war. Matted hair, bloodshot eyes, and pitted teeth were normal effects from the sand. Even the tanks and helicopters had to be washed and cleaned daily. Otherwise, the engines would fail to work in the sand.

Despite the 112,000 allied air sorties, Hussein would not retreat. But his troops were tired and frightened. Some of them ate only three spoonfuls of rice and a piece of bread every day. Before the ground war started, allied airplanes dropped leaflets into Iraq urging the Iraqis to surrender in exchange for food, blankets, and clothing. They began to defect by the thousands. When the war was over, there were 60,000 Iraqi prisoners of war (POWs).

Nothing made General Schwarzkopf angrier than the brutal treatment of allied POWs by the Iraqis. Saddam Hussein showed them wounded, beaten, and submissive on television. This inhumanity to prisoners was in violation of the Geneva Convention of 1949. Article 13 of the convention states that there will be no public display of POWs. They are to be protected from public violence and insults. Hussein further violated Article 23 of the Geneva Convention, which prohibits using POWs as human shields.

When the one American female prisoner was

finally released, Schwarzkopf met her and asked if
he could hug her. "I have thought of you and
prayed for you every night," said the general.

Early in August, Bush, Cheney, Powell, and
Schwarzkopf suspected that a ground war might be
inevitable. But they needed time to build up their
forces and get used to the sandy terrain. When all
diplomatic efforts failed to remove Iraq from
Kuwait, they selected February 23, 1991, as the
date to launch the ground war. On that day, President Mikhail Gorbachev of what was then the
Soviet Union received a message from Iraq. Hussein offered to withdraw, but with conditions. President Bush rejected that offer immediately.

The number of coalition countries participating in the air and ground war was 33 and the forces
totaled 257,900. The Iraqis had 45 divisions of
500,000 men in Kuwait and along its borders.

Meanwhile, Schwarzkopf had been devising a
ground war plan that would surprise Saddam Hussein. Many of his advisers and staff were skeptical.
They weren't sure it would work. Schwarzkopf led
the press to believe that the marines would launch
a major ground war attack on the Kuwaiti beaches.

However, Schwarzkopf secretly planned to send a mass of troops, tanks, and helicopters to the western flank of Iraq between Kuwait and Jordan. The XVIII Corps, 82nd Airborne, 3rd Armored Cavalry, the French 6th Armor, 101st Airborne, VII Corps (4 European divisions), and the 24th Infantry (mechanized) were poised for a surprise attack to squeeze the Iraqis in a pincer movement. Schwarzkopf called this a "Hail Mary" strategy. This refers to a football play where a quarterback sends all his receivers to one flank, and they run down the field to catch the pass and make a touchdown.

Saddam Hussein had his own plans for retaliation. His soldiers sabotaged a Kuwaiti oil tanker, dropping five million barrels of oil into a 35-mile stretch of the Persian Gulf, destroying wildlife and marine life. On February 24, 1991, Hussein gave the order to set fire to 732 oil wells in Kuwait. If he couldn't have Kuwait's black gold, or oil, Hussein would not let his enemies have it, either. Smoke painted the skies black for months.

On February 24, 1991, at 4:00 A.M., the ground war began, and a press blackout was enforced. The weather had been rainy and cold. Winds had been blowing into the faces of the allies. Because of the black smoke from the oil wells, flashlights had to be used to read the maps even in the middle of the day. However, during the four-day ground war, the wind shifted to the southwest and began to blow into the faces of the Iraqis. The Iraqi POWs had warned that the Iraqi Republican Guards would walk out of the flames to attack. They did walk out of the flames, but with white flags to surrender.

On February 28 at 8:00 A.M., President Bush called an end to the war after 100 hours. Since the Iraqis had been driven out of Kuwait, Bush felt the requirements of the United Nations resolutions were met. Many military and civilians argued that another day might have seen the end of Saddam Hussein. Others argued that the UN resolution was fulfilled—removing the Iraqis from Kuwait. Later, Schwarzkopf indicated that another 12 hours might have given his men time to destroy all Iraqi equipment. But President Bush was his commander-in-chief and Schwarzkopf followed the president's orders. Whatever the debate, Schwarzkopf's overall strategy will be studied as a brilliant military campaign for years to come. Already it has

The burnt-out shell of an Iraqi tank lies on a highway south of Kuwait City. The Iraqi army was quickly and decisively defeated.

been compared to Hannibal's battle of Cannae in 216 B.C. when the Carthaginians defeated the Romans.

The Kuwaitis were jubilant. They lined the streets to welcome and kiss the allies as they paraded their tanks and jeeps through Kuwait City and liberated the country from the brutality of the Iraqis.

The future of Kuwait remains uncertain. Members of the al-Sabah dynasty have ruled there since 1756. From 1899 to 1961, Kuwait was a British protectorate. In 1962, it became a constitutional monarchy. Although elections for a democratic form of government are scheduled for October 1992, there is some doubt. Kuwait's wealthy ruling emir may not want to give up his power. In the past, he bought support by giving the population large gifts of money to keep them satisfied.

After the war, General H. Norman Schwarzkopf stepped before the television cameras of the world and captured the hearts of the viewers. The press described Schwarzkopf's 51-minute performance as "the mother of all briefings." Saddam Hussein had termed the ground war as "the mother of all battles."

The allied casualties were very low: 147 killed in action and 188 through accidents and "friendly fire." However, the Iraqi deaths were believed to have been between 100,000 and 200,000. To Schwarzkopf, even one loss of life among his own troops was intolerable. He considered war a profane thing.

When asked about the military prowess of Saddam Hussein, Schwarzkopf quipped: "As far as Saddam Hussein's being a great military strategist, he is neither a strategist, nor is he schooled in the operational arts, nor is he a tactician, nor is he a general, nor is he a soldier. Other than that, he's a great military man. I want you to know that."

When General Schwarzkopf returned to the United States in June 1991, he was treated to a hero's welcome. Bantam Books signed him to a reported $5 million contract to write his autobiography. He was offered $60,000 to $100,000 to deliver speeches. Many honors have been bestowed on him, including the Medal of Freedom and invitations to the White House. Queen Elizabeth II of England came to MacDill Air Force Base for four hours in June 1991 to tap him for an honorary knighthood, which she did privately in his Central Command office. Only Prince Philip, the queen, and the Schwarzkopf family were invited for that honor. Because General Schwarzkopf is not a British subject, he was not required to kneel to receive his knighthood.

Not since General William C. Westmoreland addressed a joint session of Congress in 1967 to rally support for the Vietnam War had an American general appeared there to such an overwhelming ovation. On May 8, 1991, General H. Norman Schwarzkopf spoke with sincerity and patriotism

Retired General Norman Schwarzkopf with his family

from the podium: "We were Protestants and Catholics and Jews and Moslems and Buddhists and many other religions fighting for a common and just cause, because that's what your military is. And we were black and white and yellow and brown and red, and we noticed that when our blood was shed in the desert, it didn't separate by race; it flowed together."

Since retirement from the army in August 1991, Schwarzkopf's future has been uncertain. He has tentatively dismissed politics but might possibly consider something to do with wildlife, the environment, or education. Like his father, he has become a narrator of some television programs with historic themes. To help First Lady Barbara Bush increase literacy in the United States, he has agreed to read stories on television to children.

Whatever his future, his words: "It's a great day to be a soldier," and "It's a great day to be an American," will remind us of a great general—H. Norman Schwarzkopf, a hero with a heart.

Bibliography

Books

Anderson, Jack, and Dale Van Atta. *Stormin' Norman*. New York: Zebra Books, 1991.

Atkinson, Rick. *The Long Gray Line*. New York: Pocket Books, 1989.

Bugle Notes. West Point, N.Y.: United States Military Academy, 1957.

Cohen, Roger, and Claudio Gatti. *In the Eye of the Storm*. New York: Farrar, Strauss and Giroux, 1991.

Howitzer. West Point, N.Y.: United States Military Academy, 1917, 1956, 1958.

Morris, M. E. H. *Norman Schwarzkopf: Road to Triumph*. New York: St. Martin's Press, 1991.

Parrish, Robert D., and N. A. Andreacchio. *Schwarzkopf:*

An Insider's View of the Commander of the Victory. New York: Bantam Books, 1991.

Profile of the Army. Washington, D.C.: United States Government Printing Office, 1990.

Register of Graduates and Former Cadets. West Point, N.Y.: United States Military Academy, 1990.

Sandford, Gregory, and Richard Vigilante. *Grenada: The Untold Story*. New York: Madison Books, 1984.

Weapon Systems. Washington, D.C.: United States Government Printing Office, 1991.

Magazines and Newspapers

"The Bear." *U.S. News and World Report*, February 11, 1991, 32–42.

Bordentown Register, Centennial Edition, 1985.

Bryan, C. D. B. "Operation Desert Norm." *The New Republic*, March 11, 1991, 20–27.

De Witt, Karen, "Schwarzkopf Is Given Knighthood Without Kneeling." *The New York Times*, May 21, 1991.

"Final Lessons of Victory." *U.S. News and World Report*, March 18, 1991, 32–36.

"H. Norman Schwarzkopf." *Current Biography*, May 1991, 45–48.

Hewlett, Bill, and Linda Kramer. "Home Is the Hero." *People*, May 13, 1991, 42–47.

"How the Top Cop in Gulf Sees His Job." *U.S. News and World Report*, October 1, 1990, 34–36.

Mackenzie, Richard. "Stormin' Norman on Top." *Soldier of Fortune*, August 1991, 46–51.

Miller, Judith. "Saudi General: Norm and I Are Alike." *The New York Times*, May 5, 1991.

Murphy, John F. "Schwarzkopf: Education of a Cavalryman." *Main Line Magazine of Pennsylvania*, July/August 1991.

Nestingen, Cleo. "Sore Feet, Aching Backs, and a Right to Be Proud." *Yukon Sentinel*, August 8, 1975.

O'Malley, Sean. "That Norman, I Know Him." *Kingston Whig Standard*, May 10, 1991.

Rocawich, Linda. "The General in Charge." *The Progressive*, January 1991, 18–21.

Schwarzkopf, Brenda. "Life with Norman." *People*, Spring/Summer 1991, 6–9.

Schwarzkopf, H. Norman. "The Helmet." *Infantry*. May/June 1962, 2–4.

"A Soldier of Conscience." *Newsweek*, March 11, 1991, 32–34.

Stevenson, Jennifer. "Amid Cheers and Tears, Schwarzkopf Says Farewell." *Saint Petersburg Times*, August 10, 1991.

"Stormin' Norman on Top." *Time*, February 4, 1991, 28–30.

Triangle. New Jersey State Police, 1929.

"Unfinished Business." *U.S. News and World Report*, April 8, 1991, 18–21.

Interviews

Bahnsen, John C. Interview with author. West Point, July 1–3, 1991.

Galloway, Gerald E., Jr. Interview with author. West Point, July 3, 1991.

Grice, Martha, and Dennis Grice. Interviews with author. Fort Stewart, Georgia, September 1991.

Hausberg, Edward A. Telephone conversation with author, May 1991.

Horton, David Finch. Telephone coversation with author, May 1991.

King, Odis. Interview with author. Fort Stewart, Georgia, September 1991.

Leuer, Kenneth C. Interview with author. Columbus, Georgia, September 1991.

Morse, Ted. Telephone conversation with author, October 1991.

Palmer, Dave R. Interview with author. West Point, July 2–3, 1991.

Suddath, Leroy Newton, Jr. Interview with author. Savannah, Georgia, September 1991.

Speeches

Schwarzkopf, H. Norman. Valedictory to Valley Forge Military Academy, 1952.

——. Address at United States Military Academy, May 15, 1991.

——. Address to Joint Session of Congress, June 1, 1991.

Television

Schwarzkopf, H. Norman. Military Briefing. CNN, February 27, 1991.

——. Interview with Barbara Walters. ABC, March 1991.

——. Interview with David Frost. PBS, March 27, 1991.

——. Special. CBS, December 6, 1991.

Index

Addendum

Since this book was first published shortly after the Persian Gulf War, General Schwarzkopf has retired from the military.

One of his first projects was to write his autobiography, *It Doesn't take a Hero*. Then, he championed the cause of the Nature Conservancy and joined their board. He became chairman of the STARBRIGHT capital campaign for improving the quality of life for children with serious illnesses.

Besides working as a consultant for NBC, the General has narrated special television programs such as "D-Day."

Retired General Schwarzkopf has won numerous civilian awards and many honorary degrees. He serves as a member of the University of Richmond Board of Trustees as well as a member of the board of directors of Remington Arms Company and USA Networks, Inc.

The joys of his family and fishing continue to be his major priorities.

About the Author

Libby Hughes is a author, playwright, and lyricist. Her biographies for young adults include: Margaret Thatcher, Nelson Mandela, Colin Powell, Benazir Bhutto, Christopher Reeve, Tiger Woods, and Yitzak Rabin. Hughes edited Ginger Rogers' autobiography. Some of her plays and musicals have been produced off Broadway. She lives and writes on Cape Cod.

Printed in the United States
1342700006B/240

9 780595 255702